VOLUME 2

BOEING
777

By Jim Upton

PUBLISHERS AND WHOLESALERS

CONTENTS

THE BOEING 777

FOREWORD **4**

PREFACE **5**

CHAPTER 1 DESIGN AND MARKET NICHE **6**
THE WORLD'S MOST TECHNOLOGICALLY ADVANCED AIRLINE TRANSPORT

CHAPTER 2 AIRCRAFT FEATURES **15**
LARGEST TWIN-ENGINE AIRCRAFT IN AVIATION HISTORY

CHAPTER 3 FLIGHT TEST AND CERTIFICATION **39**
MOST TESTED AIRLINER IN AVIATION HISTORY

CHAPTER 4 AIRLINE OPERATIONS **63**
FROM A 10-SEAT AIRCRAFT TO A 10-ACROSS WIDEBODY

COLOR SECTION 777 IN DRAMATIC COLOR **65**
SCENES SELDOM SEEN

CHAPTER 5 THE 777-300 - LONGEST AIRLINER IN THE WORLD **82**
THE STRETCHED 777-300

CHAPTER 6 THE FUTURE **93**
A 30 TO 50 YEAR VENTURE

APPENDICES **98**

SIGNIFICANT DATES **100**
KEY DATES IN THE HISTORY OF THE BOEING 777

FOREWORD

Participating in the design, production and flight testing of the 777 has been one of the most exciting and meaningful highlights of my 33-year career as a flight test engineer. As Jim Upton so ably describes, the development of the 777 represents a huge leap forward in technology and in the way the industry builds and tests airplanes.

As Flight Test Chief Engineer of the 777 program, I participated in the design of the 777 before we even decided to call it by that name. It is this "working together" concept that has been the key ingredient in the success of this project. I was responsible for the flight test program, but I and everyone else contributed to the design and production process through the working together concept.

The investment we made then, is paying off now, in the flight test world as well as with the airlines. Just outside my office window, the latest derivative of the 777, the -300 model, takes off for flight testing. Compared to the original 777 program, we are realizing even higher flight rates with less cost. Jim doesn't miss a beat in capturing these significant details accurately and completely.

I first met Jim in 1975 at the experimental test pilot's office in Lancaster, California during a technical council meeting of the Society of Flight Test Engineers. I was impressed with his incredible knowledge of airplanes and with his enthusiasm for flight test. In the course of our ongoing participation on Society boards and committees, we have stayed in contact every year since.

We who have worked and played with airplanes through the years count Jim as a treasured friend and we are thankful for his highly successful transition to an aviation writing career.

Cliff Moore
Director, Boeing Commercial Airplane
Group Flight Test Engineering
1998

Cliff Moore over looks the flight line at the flight test center located on Boeing Field in Seattle. Cliff was Flight Test Chief Engineer for the 777 program during the original 777 development and currently is Director of Boeing Commerical Airplane Group Flight Test Engineering. (Boeing)

PREFACE

Boeing's history began in 1916 in the "Red Barn," now part of the Museum of Flight in Seattle. A biplane called the B & W, a single engine float plane, was the first aircraft built in the original manufacturing building.

Boeing's current wide-body aircraft manufacturing facility, where the 777 is built, is large enough to house Disneyland along with twelve acres of covered parking. In sharp contrast to the original red barn, the main building in Everett, Washington is eleven stories tall. By volume it is the largest in the world with assembly positions for twenty-eight aircraft.

The 777 is a fascinating aircraft to examine in detail. With all the new technology incorporated into this aircraft, there are many firsts for an airliner, ranging from size of the powerplants to new comfort features for the passengers and advanced features in the cockpit. As the most tested airliner

in aviation history, the unique flight test operations should be of interest to the reader. This volume of Airliner Tech starts with design and progresses chronologically through aircraft features, flight test and certification, airline operations, and details of the latest version of the 777, the stretched -300. The Boeing 777 book also gives a glimpse into the future.

Each time a new acronym is presented in a chapter, a description follows such as ETOPS (Extended-range Twin-engine OPerationS). Sub-headings help in linking text with corresponding photographs and technical illustrations.

Finally, a publication like this would not be possible without the help of many people. I would like to thank the following for their contributions in making this book possible:

At Boeing Commercial Airplane Group: Cliff Moore, Bob Dawes, Andy Hammer, Jeff Goedhard, Denise

The original Boeing Airplane Company building is now located at the Museum of Flight in Seattle, Washington. In addition to the interesting aircraft displayed, the interior offices and engineering design area have been restored to their early day configuration. (Author)

Blangy, Ron Schaevitz, all of Flight Test Engineering, John Kvasnosky and Dave Copeland of Customer Services Division, Gary Vassallo of ETOPS Programs, Kirsti Dunn and Ida Hawkins of Everett-Site Media Communications. Phil Schultz and Jim Stump, at General Electric Aircraft Engines, Mark Sullivan of Pratt & Whitney Engines, Marsha Hodson at Rolls Royce, Audra Grigaliunas of United Airlines, Sandy Gardiner of British Airways, Tom Friedo at All Nippon Airways, Lilian Lai of Cathay Pacific Airways, Bob Gano at Japan Air Lines, Kandy Akina at Singapore Airlines, Emilia Reed of Ball Aerospace & Technologies, Dave Elston and Ceile Plonski of AlliedSignal, and Jennifer Villarreal of Smith Industries Stephen L. Griffin and Tom Pesch for their photos. My thanks to Paul Stevenson for his review, and to Nicholas A. Veronico for his direction, review and helpful suggestions. Special thanks to my wife Carol for her research, editing, and supportive patience during this time intensive project.

Jim Upton
1998

An aerial view of the Boeing wide-body manufacturing plant in Everett Washington. The final assembly is accomplished in the white roof building in the center of the photo. (Boeing)

Why another airliner design? The Boeing 777 family was designed to fill a niche between 300 and 500 seats. Market-demand sized, shaped, and launched this newest member of the Boeing family. Designed to be the most efficient airline market solution for any range, with virtually the same aircraft, the 777 offers a choice of models that share the same flight crew type rating. This is an attractive feature for air-lines since the costs of recurrence training, transition training, and pilot pool size can be significant. This air-craft fits between the current Boeing 767-300 and the 747-400 in both size and range. The Triple 7 is designed to meet changing market demands through cabin flexibility, range capa-bility, and multiple sizes of the same aircraft. Cabin flexibility includes the ability to move seats, luggage bins, lavatories, or galleys to various loca-tions in the aircraft that have built-in structural and hook up provisions. These "Flex Zones" allow the airline to make cabin configuration changes to meet changing market demands in hours instead of days or weeks.

Boeing's first all-new design since 1978, when the 757 and 767 first began, the 777 is currently built in three models. The -200 is the initial model (sometimes referred to as the "A-Market" model). It seats 305 to 440

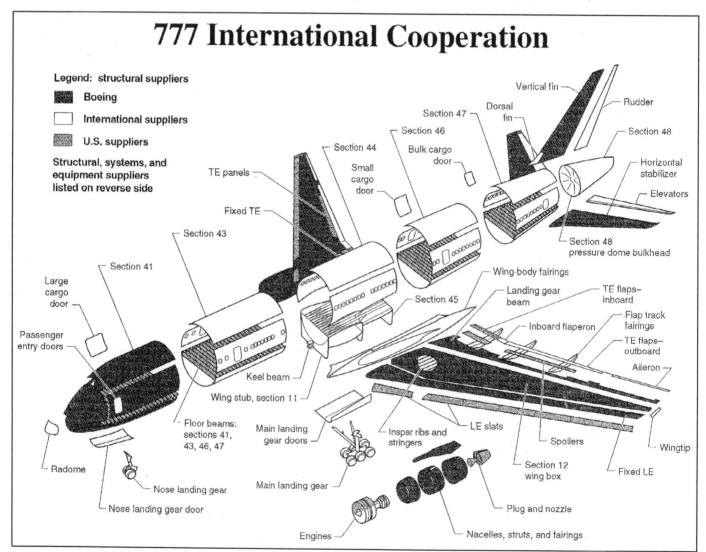

777 International Cooperation

Legend: structural suppliers
- Boeing
- International suppliers
- U.S. suppliers

Structural, systems, and equipment suppliers listed on reverse side

Dimensions and general arrangement of the 777-200. Its size and range capability places it right in between the 767-300 and the 747-400. (Boeing)

The 777 Is Sized Between the 767 and 747
Business Class Shown

198.0
(5.03m)

244.0
(6.20m)

255.5
(6.49m)

6 abreast

7 abreast

7 abreast

LD-2 LD-2

LD-3 LD-3

LD-1 LD-1

767

777

747

Size Comparison

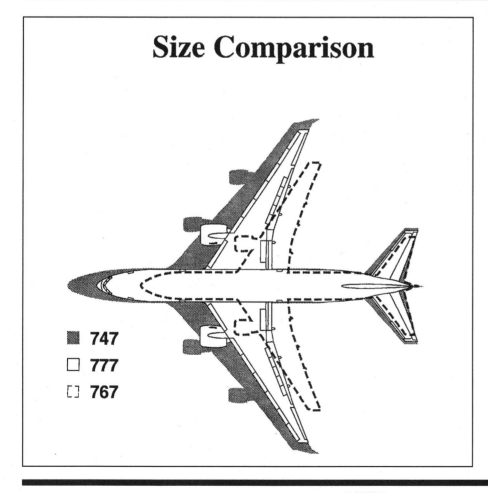

■ **747**
☐ **777**
[] **767**

Cross section comparing the 777 to the 767 and 747. In a business class arrangement of seven seats across, the 777 is very similar to the 747. (Boeing)

This top view shows an interesting size comparison between the 747, 777, and 767. Wing span, length, and fuselage diameter put the 777-200 between the 747 and 767. Passenger capacity is also in the middle, between the two aircraft. (Boeing)

passengers and has a maximum range of approximately 4,800 nautical miles. The -200 Increased Gross Weight (IGW) model, known as the "B-Market" model, is the same size as the -200 but has internal structural changes for a higher gross weight takeoff with more fuel, giving it an approximate maximum range of 7,400 nautical miles. The latest model, the -300, is the largest twin-jet airliner in the world. Stretched 33 feet from the initial -200,

Business Class seating is seven across in a 2-3-2 configuration. Notice the headroom in all of the seat locations. The carry on luggage bins are designed to be up and out of the way when closed, but are still easily accessible when they open and pull down. (Boeing)

to 242 feet 4 inches, it carries between 328 and 550 passengers. Its maximum range is 5,600 nautical miles. Future 777 models are currently in the product development study phase. They include cargo versions and further increased range versions.

Boeing held intensive discussions with a number of carriers, including United Airlines, All Nippon Airways, British Airways, Japan Airlines, and Cathay Pacific, to define and develop the new aircraft's configuration. These airlines represented a full range of operations in terms of route structure, traffic loads, and service frequency. Their input to the design process helped ensure that the final product had the broadest possible application to the needs of the world's airlines.

Customer dialog also resulted in the consensus that many items traditionally offered as optional or special-request features on other aircraft should be standard equipment, since they were so frequently specified by most airlines. About eighty such items, including satellite communications

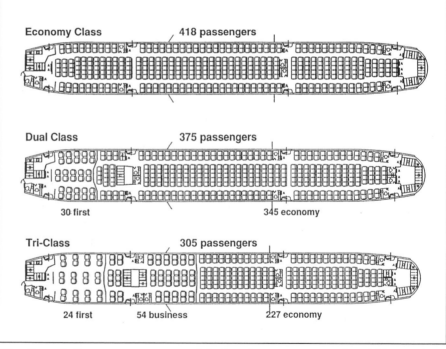

777 Flexible Seating

Economy Class   418 passengers

Dual Class   375 passengers

30 first   345 economy

Tri-Class   305 passengers

24 first   54 business   227 economy

"Flex Zones" allow rearrangement of the interior to accommodate 305 to 418 passengers on the 777-200. Flex Zones make it possible to change and move the seats, galleys, and lavatories. This is possible because structural, electrical, and plumbing provisions have been designed into the aircraft. (Boeing)

United Airlines Influence on 777 Design

- ▶ Application of lower wing panel splice joint sealant
- ▶ Access panel latches
- ▶ Passenger reading light replaceability
- ▶ Unpressurized area wire gauge increase
- ▶ Translating ceiling stowage bins
- ▶ Ceiling stowage compartments at doors 1 and 4
- ▶ Nickel plated fuel tank wiring
- ▶ Refueling panel location
- ▶ Flight deck altitude select knob
- ▶ 'Towbarless' tractor nose gear design
- ▶ Main landing gear axle sleeves
- ▶ Overwing refueling ports deletion

Airline participation played an important part in the design of the 777. This illustration shows a number of United Airlines contributions. (United Airlines)

and Global Positioning Systems (GPS), are now basic to the aircraft. This reduces variability during design and production while providing the airlines with a more economical equipment package.

From the passenger's viewpoint the 777 is large and roomy, with dual, wide aisles, plenty of head and hip room, space for maneuvering, and roomy overhead luggage storage bins that are out of the way, yet within easy reach. Passengers also notice the reduced noise level of quieter engines. The entertainment system is selected by individual airlines and can include items like individual displays at each seat, which on United Airlines (for example) have six channels of video, nineteen channels of CD quality audio,

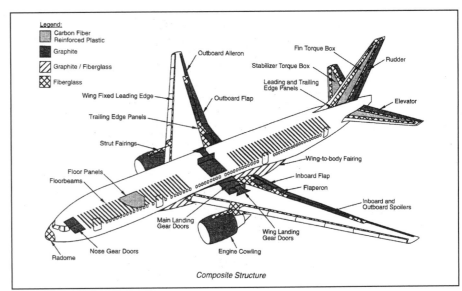

Legend:
- Carbon Fiber Reinforced Plastic
- Graphite
- Graphite / Fiberglass
- Fiberglass

Outboard Aileron · Fin Torque Box · Stabilizer Torque Box · Rudder · Wing Fixed Leading Edge · Outboard Flap · Leading and Trailing Edge Panels · Elevator · Trailing Edge Panels · Strut Fairings · Wing-to-body Fairing · Floor Panels · Inboard Flap · Floorbeams · Flaperon · Inboard and Outboard Spoilers · Main Landing Gear Doors · Wing Landing Gear Doors · Nose Gear Doors · Engine Cowling · Radome

Composite Structure

Weight-saving advanced composite materials accounted for over nine percent of the total 777 structure. Composites have good resistance to fatigue, corrosion, and impact damage. (Boeing)

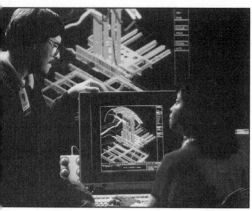

CATIA 3-D software was used in the digital design of the 777 to eliminate the requirement for hard mockups. Normally, in a two-dimensional design process, a metal mock-up of the aircraft is built. All components are then installed in the metal three-dimensional world to check for interferences. (Boeing)

Wind tunnel models helped validate and refine 777 computational models. Wind tunnel engineer Dan Panich checks the model before a wind tunnel run. (Boeing)

video games, and telecommunication services.

DESIGN

In 1989, Boeing contacted a number of airlines to research their requirements for a new airliner. This airliner, originally designated the 767-X, evolved into a completely new model, the Boeing 777, when it was determined that airlines really required a new aircraft. From the manufacturer's perspective, building a new aircraft instead of modifying an existing one would allow the use of new design and manufacturing processes. This would result in new capabilities and more efficient methods of design and manufacturing. It would also start an entire family of airliners to eventually replace early 747s.

Boeing used a fundamentally new approach to construct the 777. Design/Build Teams (DBTs) were established to develop each element of the aircraft's airframe and systems. All of the different specialties involved in aircraft development were co-located and worked concurrently as teams, sharing knowledge rather than just applying skills sequentially. DBTs included designers, manufacturing

Forward fuselage section of 777-200 WA101 during assembly operations at the Everett, Washington factory. This was the stage of construction on the first 777 on November 4, 1994. (Boeing/Bob Carnahan)

representatives, tooling and engineering, finance specialists, customers, and suppliers' all working jointly to create the aircraft's parts and systems.

Concurrent engineering techniques were used extensively on the new design, resulting in a fifty-percent reduction in engineering changes due to design errors. This in turn led to a significant reduction in the defects that reached the factory floor. Costs and delivery schedules were both favorably affected.

All affected engineering disciplines were involved in problem resolution; consequently, problems were resolved long before they reached the production phase. The 100-percent digital design was the industry's first. Digital mockups and preassembly using CATIA 3-D software (a trademark of Dassault Systems SA) helped the DBTs integrate all systems and components, and check for interferences. This was accomplished without having to build hard mock-ups. Designing in parallel reduced design-cycle time and improved quality, since more alternatives could be evaluated. These integrated product-teams reduced organizational barriers and improved communication, resulting in the commonly heard phrase *Working Together*, used to describe the team effort. The first 777 to be rolled out was named *Working Together*.

AIRLINE PARTICIPATION

The active participation of airline customer representatives in the 777's design process was a major change. Approximately 300 airline employees were co-located at Boeing and integrated into the DBTs. Japan Air Lines (JAL) had forty engineers working on the 777; some in Seattle, and others at home in Japan. One of the areas they affected was the fifteen-volume maintenance manual set. It was a challenge to design manuals in English that would be understandable in non-English locations.

When representatives of the "Working Together" airlines were asked what

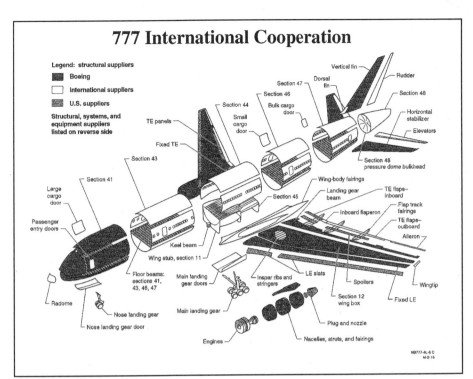

Assembly breakdown illustration of the 777. Structural suppliers are shown by shading legend. (Boeing)

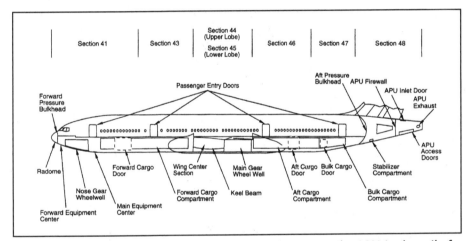

Major fuselage components and compartment locations. The APU, in the tail of the aircraft, is in an unpressurized area. Eight passenger doors on the 777-200 are shown. There are ten passenger doors on the stretched -300. (Boeing)

they wanted in the 777, Gordon McKinzie of United Airlines replied, "We were looking for better seat-mile costs in an airplane to replace our DC-10s. In choosing the 777 over the MD-11 and A330, we weighted mission capability highest. We weighted the cockpits of the airplanes and new technology lowest."

Kenichi Hashimoto of All Nippon Airways commented, "We wanted an airplane for domestic flights to replace Lockheed L-1011s and Boeing 747s. We

are always looking for higher reliability. I'm convinced the Triple 7 will have much higher reliability because we participated in the entire design process."

Barry Gosnold of British Airways said, "The 777 best met our requirements for a medium-size wide-body airplane that would be flexible and extremely reliable as a replacement for our wide-body tri-jets. We wanted very good seat-mile costs, high passenger appeal, and a very high level of dis-

Mid-fuselage section of the 777-200 during move to the next assembly position. Note the circular shape of the fuselage. (Boeing/Bob Carnahan)

A 14-ton left wing for the first 777 is lifted from its production tool. It is being moved to the cradle on the floor where internal and external work will be completed. The final assembly line for the smaller 767 appears in the background. (Boeing)

patch reliability from Day One, coupled with ETOPS capability."

Tadao Sakai of Japan Airlines commented, "We put the top priority on high levels of safety and maintainability. Our first three airplanes will be for expansion of domestic routes. Probably number four will go on relatively short-range international routes."

Examples of design impact by participating airlines include Cathay Pacific's influence on the 747-like dimensions of the cabin sizing, and United Airlines' desire for the stowage bins over the center row of passenger seats to swing down-and-out for easy access from the aisles. On exterior matters, United had Boeing shift the fueling panel closer to the ground

AIRLINER**TECH**
S E R I E S

because the original location was too high for the airline's fueling trucks. All Nippon worked with Boeing on numerous details, including a redesign of the toilet seats to eliminate the loud bang when the seat was dropped, accomplished by adding a damping mechanism to close the lid quietly.

British Airways suggested a way to reconfigure the aft galleys to make space for two lavatories moved from elsewhere in the aircraft. This freed up room for four additional seats at no extra cost, without any adverse impact on service to the passengers. Japan Airlines suggested a number of improvements in the cockpit displays for flight management and aircraft systems information.

777 TECHNOLOGY

Many new technologies were incorporated in the design and building of the Triple 7. New generation high-bypass ratio engines provide forty per-cent more thrust and better fuel con-

The center fuselage section and wing are moved to the final body join position. All major aircraft structures are brought together in factory tooling and aligned with a new computer-operated laser alignment and leveling system, providing precise alignment from nose to tail and wing-tip to wing-tip. Employees will permanently fasten the structures and continue integrating and installing systems, landing gear, wing flaps, and fairings. (Boeing)

Final assembly position for the 777 at the Everett, Washington wide-body factory, where the engines and final systems are installed. All exterior aluminum surfaces are coated with a thin layer of green vinyl to guard against scratches. Vinyl is applied early in the assembly process and is removed just before painting the aircraft. (Boeing)

sumption than previous engines. These engines also have lower community noise levels than previous designs. Advanced composite materials are used for nine percent of the structure of the aircraft and improved structural dura-bility is provided through the design and use of new alloys. Other new tech-nology items include the six-wheeled main landing gear with its single main strut design. This design improves pavement loading with greater growth potential than landing gear with multi-ple struts. The fly-by-wire flight control system, with its pilot-friendly features and flexibility, requires less mainte-nance at reduced weight than a conven-tional mechanical-control system. Flat-panel cockpit displays bring the latest technology to the flight station.

Extensive wind tunnel testing was used to resolve a number of the aerodynamic design issues for the wing. These early efforts resulted in the 777 having the most aerodynami-cally efficient airfoil ever developed for subsonic commercial aviation. New reliability design and testing resulted in early ETOPS (Extended-range Twin-engine OPerationS) certification. United Airlines started its first revenue service with ETOPS approval, greatly extending the number of routes that the company could fly on fleet introduction. Integrated avionics and the use of the ARINC 629 (Aeronautical Radio Incorporated) data bus allowed faster communication between the many Line Replaceable Units (LRU's), using fewer wires.

MANUFACTURING

The skills and resources of a number of international aerospace companies contributed to the 777's design and production. Firms in Europe, Canada, Asia/Pacific, and the United States provided components and portions of the structure to Boeing. The international cooperation included suppliers for structural components, systems, equipment, and engines.

The Japanese aerospace industry is the largest single overseas manufacturing participant. Led by Mitsubishi Heavy Industries, Kawasaki Heavy Industries, and Fuji Heavy Industries, this group of companies is continuing a long-standing business relationship with Boeing. Together, these firms helped design and build about twenty percent of the airframe structure.

Assembly takes place at Boeing's Everett, Washington plant. Enclosing 472 million cubic feet of space, the main assembly building is 11 stories tall and covers 98.3 acres. By volume, it is the largest building in the world.

View in the Everett Washington factory shows the 777 final body join position in the foreground and final assembly position in the background. This position is the last position before roll out to the paint hangar. (Boeing)

Three topcoats of white paint were applied to the first 777 in the paint hangar. After curing of the final coat, the aircraft was masked and blue and red markings were added. Approximately 35 painters worked five days to apply 586 pounds of paint. (Boeing)

Aircraft Features

Boeing's 777 has a number of unique features. It is the largest twinjet flying today and, following the recent first flight of the -300, is also the longest commercial jetliner in the world. The wing design features a long span (199 feet 11 inches) and improves the plane's ability to climb quickly and cruise at higher altitudes, improving fuel efficiency. It offers more payload and range capabilities than competing models, with lower operating costs.

CABIN

Depending on the desired seating layout, the Boeing -200 can be configured from six to ten abreast in the spacious cabin. Flex Zones allow airlines

United's Connoisseur Class has a seven-across seat configuration. Window seats have stand up room, and the center row overhead carry-on luggage bins are easily accessible, yet out of the way when closed. (United Airlines)

Cutaway drawing of the 777 shows the spacious, flexible interior of the wide-body twinjet. The turbofan engine nacelle has a diameter equal to the fuselage diameter of the 737. (Boeing)

to easily move galleys and lavatories to match seating-arrangement changes. The overhead bins for carry-on luggage are a new innovation. The contoured bins, which protrude from the walls in other aircraft, are slanted at a 45-degree angle toward the ceiling. As a result, passengers on the window aisle can stand straight up without bumping their heads. There are also bins for the center aisle seats. Flight attendant controllable systems include cabin temperature and lighting.

ENGINES

Design thrust requirements made it necessary for engine manufacturers to develop a fuel-efficient, high-thrust power plant that would produce 15,000-30,000 pounds greater thrust than any available engines. A high reliability level (i.e., a low in-flight shutdown rate) was needed at airline entry into service to satisfy ETOPS

PW4084 engine on 777 WA003 with the engine cowl doors open. The first five aircraft built, WA001 through WA005, were all powered by P&W engines. (Boeing/Bob Carnahan)

(Extended-range Twin-engine OPerationS) reliability criteria. Consequently, the engine technology used in the 777 would need to combine proven technology with new technology that had been proven by a rigorous testing program to accomplish power plant goals.

These goals were accomplished through higher bypass ratios, increased overall pressure ratios, improved thermal efficiency, and increased reliability of individual components. Additionally, noise and emission levels were lowered in anticipation of new, more restrictive regulations. Customers may choose to power their new 777s with engines from Pratt & Whitney, General Electric, or Rolls Royce.

Pratt & Whitney

Pratt & Whitney builds the PW4000-series engine. This family of engines incorporates a 112-inch diameter fan and has thrust ratings from 74,000 to 89,000 pounds. The initial PW4084 engine ordered by United Airlines for the first 777 was certified at 84,600 pounds thrust, and rated at 77,200 pounds thrust.

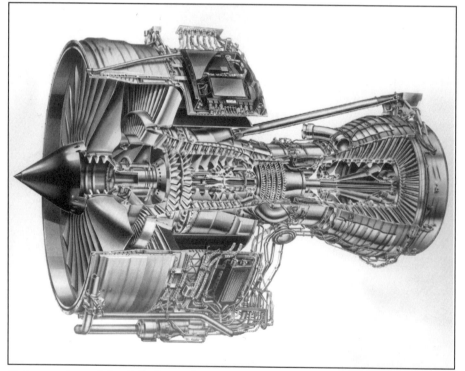

Cutaway view of the Rolls-Royce Trent 800 engine. Thrust ratings on the Trent 800 series engines range from 75,000 pounds to 92,000 pounds. (Rolls-Royce)

PW4000 112-INCH FAN ENGINE

Cutaway view of the Pratt & Whitney PW4000 Turbofan engine, one of three engine manufacturer options on the 777. Thrust ratings for the PW4000 series engines range from 74,000 pounds to 98,000 pounds. (Pratt & Whitney)

Pratt & Whitney PW4000 engine, including engine gearbox details. Locations of the backup generator and the permanent magnet alternator on the gearbox are shown. Positions for the starter, hydraulic pump, lube and scavenge pump, and Integrated Drive Generator(IDG) are also shown. (Boeing)

Pratt & Whitney began work on the PW4084 in 1989. The company had decided to build a derivative of its PW4000 engine instead of designing an all-new powerplant. Engineers modified the PW4000's design to handle a forty percent increase in thrust and fifteen percent increase in temperature. PW4084 was completed on July 1, 1992 and, barely a month later, run at thrust ratings in excess of 90,000 pounds. Shortly thereafter, the engine was run up to over 100,000 pounds to prove its robustness and ability to grow into future requirements.

During the nearly two-year certification process, PW4084s were put through the toughest testing ever devised for a commercial aircraft engine. Twenty-two engines were dedicated to the testing process. For certification the engines were run more than 2,500 hours, the equivalent of 6,000 flight cycles - takeoff, climb, cruise, descent, and landing. In one test, a dynamite charge was used to blow off one of the engine's massive fan blades at full power. The force of impact on the engine's case equaled a full-size car hitting a brick wall at eighty miles an hour - but the engine had to absorb the damage and contain

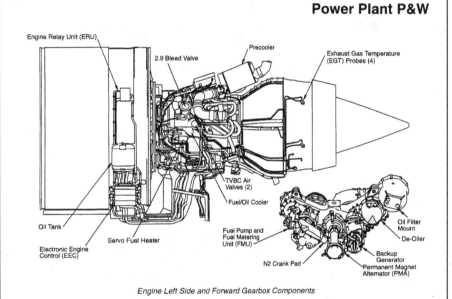

Power Plant P&W

Engine Left Side and Forward Gearbox Components

Engine Right Side and Aft Gearbox Components

PW4084 engines being installed on the 777. Engine installation occurs at the final assembly position of the production line. United Airlines was the launch customer for the Pratt & Whitney engines, and the initial launch customer for the 777. (Pratt & Whitney)

the blade fragments within the engine case. In another test, slabs of ice were forced into the engine and it had to operate in a simulated rainstorm equal to rainfall of twenty-eight inches an hour - something that has a one-in-a-billion chance of occurring!

Following the completion of the ground certification process, five Pratt-powered 777s went through the most grueling flight test and certification program in aviation history. These aircraft flew for 3,100 hours and 3,400 cycles. More than 1,500 items were checked almost 27,000 times! Engines were shut down in mid-flight, and re-lit. Takeoffs were accomplished on one engine.

The current series of P&W 4000

engines consists of the PW4084, certified in April 1994 with a takeoff rated thrust of 86,760 pounds; the PW4090, certified in June 1996 with a takeoff rated thrust of 91,790 pounds; and the PW4098, under development. The PW4098 is planned for certification in January 1998 with a takeoff rated thrust of 98,000 pounds.

General Electric

General Electric builds the GE90 series engine. This family of engines has thrust ratings from 76,000 to 92,000 pounds. The GE90-85B, derated to 76,000 pounds thrust, powers the 777-200 models. The GE90-92B, derated to 90,000 pounds thrust, pow-

ers the -200 IGW (Increased Gross Weight) models. The GE90 is the largest fan jet engine in the world: its 123-inch diameter fan is approximately equal to the fuselage diameter of a Boeing 727.

GE's most extensive engine development program included one of the most extensive ground and flight test programs ever undertaken by an engine manufacturer. A total of thirteen GE90 engines were used in ground tests. Seven engines were operated at more than 100,000 pounds thrust, one of which achieved a record-breaking 110,000 pounds of thrust. GE performed 228 hours of flight testing with its specially modified 747 flying test-bed before the

The Trent 800 in preparation for testing at Rolls-Royce. The white stripes on the spinner at the front of the fan blades are to discourage birds from flying into the engine inlet. Birds apparently mistake the dark inlet cavity for a cave entrance. (Rolls-Royce)

GE90 was flown on the 777.

Although the GE90 is basically a new engine, it incorporates technology from the very successful CF6 and CFM56 engine families. It is designed for high propulsive and high thermal efficiency: a very reliable engine that produces the needed thrust at good fuel efficiencies.

General Electric's design, manufacturing, and revenue sharing partners are Snecma of France, IHI of Japan, and FiatAvio of Italy. British Airways was the launch customer for the GE90.

Rolls Royce Trent

Rolls Royce builds the Trent 800 series engine. This family of engines

has thrust ratings from 75,000 to 92,000 pounds. The Trent engine design is derived from the reliable RB211 family of three-shaft engines (this term refers to the three concentric shafts coupling the turbine and compressor sections of the engine).

Various models of the engine use a different data-entry plug, or software change, to modify the rating of the engine. This feature allows future higher-thrust engines to be intermixed with current power plants, increasing flexibility for operators. A Trent 8102 engine (102,000 pounds thrust) could be installed on a 777 with a Trent 892 (92,000 pounds thrust), for example, because the data-entry plug limits the higher-thrust engine to 92,000-pound thrust operation. This could reduce the number of spares an airline operator needs to maintain a 777 fleet that uses several engine versions.

The 110-inch diameter fan at the front of the engine uses wide-chord fan blades to produce about seventy-five percent of the Trent engine's thrust. It has a 6.5 bypass ratio and 40:1 pressure ratio. Load on a fan blade at take-off is almost 100 tons: the equivalent of hanging a main-line diesel locomotive on each blade. There are ninety-two high-pressure turbine blades in the engine. Each one generates about 750 horsepower. Efficient control of engine operation is obtained through the use of a Digital Engine Control (DEC).

Trent 800 engines on the Rolls-Royce build-line in Derby, England. This is the final assembly line for the engines. Notice the accessories mounted on the bottom of the fan case. (Rolls-Royce)

Rolls-Royce Trent engine installed on RA001, Boeing's 747-100 flying test bed. Fan cowl doors have a powered door opening system because of their massive size. (Boeing/Bob Carnahan)

Thai Airways was the launch customer for the Rolls Royce Trent Engine.

APU

The Auxiliary Power Unit (APU) performs a number of critical functions in the operation of the aircraft. This 730-pound turbine engine, mounted in the tail, drives a 120 kVA (kiloVolt-Ampere) generator and centrifugal load compressor that can provide all needed electrical and pneumatic power. It is easily accessed for maintenance through large clamshell doors in the bottom of the tail cone. Inlet air enters the APU through a door on the top and exhausts through a port on the aft left side of the tail cone.

AlliedSignal Aerospace built the 331-500 APU specifically for the Boeing 777. In flight, the APU provides a backup source for electrical and pneumatic power. It produces approximately 1,250-shaft hp and is capable of starting

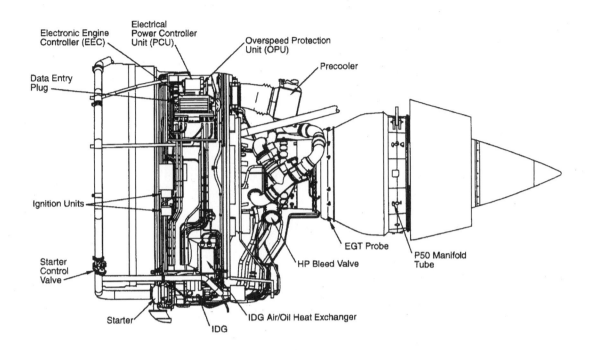

Electronic Engine Controller (EEC)

Electrical Power Controller Unit (PCU)

Overspeed Protection Unit (OPU)

Precooler

Data Entry Plug

Ignition Units

Starter Control Valve

Starter

IDG

IDG Air/Oil Heat Exchanger

HP Bleed Valve

EGT Probe

P50 Manifold Tube

Engine Left Side

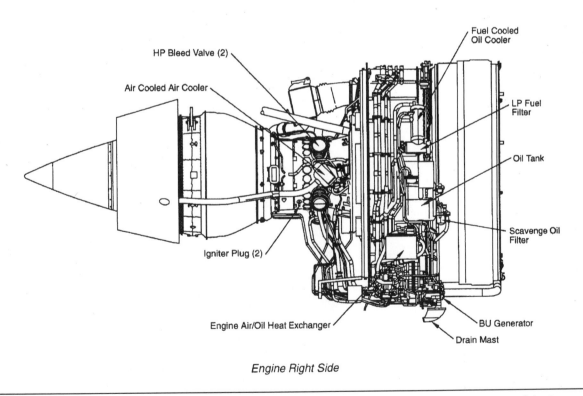

Fuel Cooled Oil Cooler

HP Bleed Valve (2)

Air Cooled Air Cooler

LP Fuel Filter

Oil Tank

Scavenge Oil Filter

Igniter Plug (2)

Engine Air/Oil Heat Exchanger

Drain Mast

BU Generator

Engine Right Side

Engine details on the Rolls-Royce Trent. Notice the fan case location for accessories like the starter and the Integrated Drive Generator(IDG), compared to the gearbox location for these items on the P&W engine. This comparison shows differences in the way individual engine manufacturers design their engines. (Boeing)

Boeing's 747 flying test bed, RA001, landing at Boeing Field after a test flight with the Trent 800 engine on the left inboard position. RA001 was the first 747 built. It was leased from the Museum of Flight for the engine testing. (Rolls-Royce)

guide vane control, data storage, protective shutdowns, bite/fault reporting, and APU indications.

The APUC also provides automated functions that communicate with other aircraft systems over the ARINC 629 digital data bus. This advance in digital communication has increased overall system ability to meet the demands of the aircraft. It can anticipate changes in pneumatic demand by monitoring flight deck commands and valve positions, for example, and respond quickly and effectively to these direct inputs. The APU starts automatically when the loss of other primary electrical power is sensed, providing 120 kVA of backup power immediately, without any action by the pilot.

AlliedSignal performed extensive testing on the 331-500 APU and delivering a full generator load of 120 kilowatts up to an altitude of 43,100 feet. The APU's load compressor pneumatic output operates the air-driven hydraulic pumps up to their limit of 19,000 feet and is also available for main engine starting and cabin pressurization up to 22,000 feet. Additionally, the pneumatic output from the APU can be used as a source for wing anti-ice, and by the Environmental Control Systems (ECS) for air conditioning. On the ground, the APU can provide electrical and pneumatic power in locations where there are no electrical ground carts or ground-air sources.

The 331-500's dual start system is a novel innovation that includes both air turbine and electric starters. The air turbine starter is driven by either bleed-air from the engine or a ground start cart. If neither source is available, the electric starter is selected. Starter selection is made automatically by the Auxiliary Power Unit Controller (APUC), a computer located in the aft end of the cabin (the start source can also be selected manually in the cockpit). The APUC controls a number of functions, including starting and ignition, fuel control, surge control, inlet

Singapore Airlines Rolls-Royce Trent 800 powered 777. The massive size of the turbofan engine is apparent with the technician standing in the inlet. (Rolls-Royce)

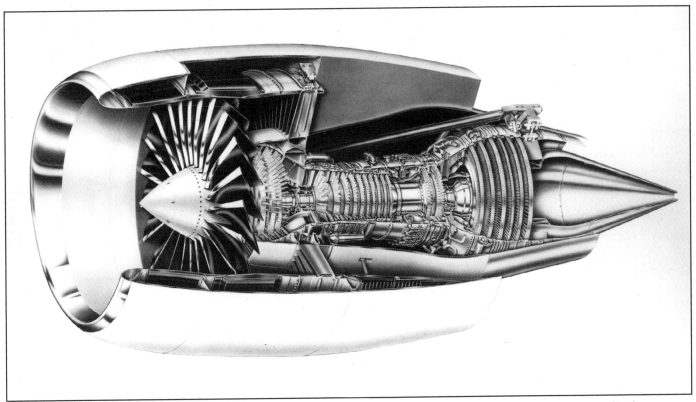

Cutaway view of the GE90 propulsion system shows the GE90 high bypass turbofan engine, nacelle, and nozzle. Thrust ratings for the GE90 series engines range from 76,000 pounds to 92,000 pounds. (GE Aircraft Engines)

prior to first flight. Its development test program began in February 1992. It accumulated approximately 12,500 hours and 22,000 starts prior to entry into revenue service in June 1995. After TSO (Technical Service Order) approval by the FAA in November 1993, additional testing was completed to facilitate the requirements for out of the box ETOPS approval for the 777. The high reliability of the APU and its systems contributed to overall ETOPS approval for the 777's entry into service with United Airlines.

RAT

The Ram Air Turbine (RAT) is a source of emergency electrical and hydraulic power for the fly-by-wire flight control system. It consists of a retractable turbine that drives a generator and a hydraulic pump. The two-bladed variable pitch turbine is forty-two inches in diameter and maintains approximately 4,500 RPM down to an airspeed of 115 knots.

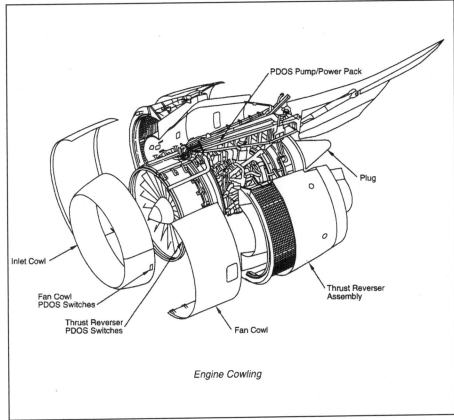

Engine cowling showing the Powered Door Opening System (PDOS) and thrust reversers. Pump and power pack for the PDOS is located at the top of the engine pylon. (Boeing)

The RAT is stowed in the wing-to-body fairing behind the right wheel well. In normal flight conditions, the RAT is in the stowed or retracted position. Less than a minute after an AC power loss on the aircraft, the RAT extends automatically and its 7.5 kVA generator begins providing power to all of the standby system loads. The RAT's hydraulic pump provides a ten gallon-per-minute flow, at 2,850 psi, to the flight control system.

The RAT will automatically extend in the air if there is a loss of hydraulic pressure, a loss of rpm from both engines, or a loss of electrical power to the left and right transfer busses. The pilot has manual control of RAT extension.

HYDRAULIC POWER SYSTEM

The 777 has three independent 3,000 psi hydraulic systems. The left engine powers the left system, the APU powers the center system, and the right engine powers the right system. All three systems supply pressure to the primary flight controls, providing triple

A technician prepares a GE90 engine for shipment at the GE Aircraft Engines test complex near Peebles, Ohio. Note the size of the fan compared to the technician. (GE Aircraft Engines)

redundancy for this critical function. Automatic prioritization is accorded to the primary flight controls, high lift

Checking the GE90 engine during ETOPS qualification. The hold open bars are a safety feature in addition to the Powered Door Opening System. (GE Aircraft Engines)

devices, and landing gear, in that order. The RAT is on the center system. As discussed earlier, it supplies an emergency source of hydraulic pressure to operate the primary flight controls in the event of the loss of all other pumps.

The left and right systems each have an Engine Driven Pump (EDP) for primary and an Alternating Current Motor Pump (ACMP) for demand. The center hydraulic system has two ACMPs for primary and two Air Driven Pumps (ADPs) for demand. Primary pumps operate constantly: demand pumps operate only when there is a large hydraulic flow requirement. The three types of hydraulic pumps (engine driven, AC, and air) differ mainly in their power source. Engine-driven pumps have a geared mechanical drive from the engine gearbox, while alternating current motor pumps are driven by an electric motor. Air-driven pumps use an air drive assembly with a turbine that uses the aircraft's pneumatic system. Using three different types of power sources for the hydraulic pumps provides greater redundancy to the hydraulic system.

Boeing 777 twinjet powered by GE90 engines. The impressive size of the engines compared to the wide-body fuselage is evident in this head on, in-flight view. (GE Aircraft Engines)

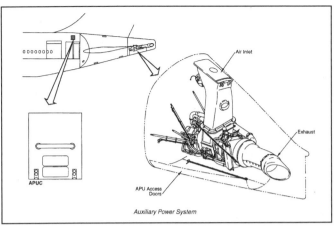

The APU location is shown in the tail of the 777. Clam-shell maintenance access doors are located on the bottom of the tail, with the air inlet through a door at the top of the tail cone, and exhaust through a port on the left side. (Boeing)

AlliedSignal Aerospace 331-500 Auxiliary Power Unit (APU) from the right side. This view shows various accessories including the dual start system, consisting of the air turbine starter and the electric starter. Two types of starters are part of the built-in redundancy designed from the start to support ETOPS qualification of the 1250 horsepower APU. (AlliedSignal)

The servicing of the three systems is accomplished from a single location in the ground-servicing bay behind the right wheel well. A selector valve chooses the reservoir to be serviced and a quantity gauge shows the fluid level of the selected reservoir. Servicing can be accomplished through the manual on-board pump or through a pressure connection.

The redundancy and reliability of the hydraulic system was a big contributor to ETOPS out-of-the-box approval.

ELECTRICAL POWER SYSTEMS

The Boeing 777's electrical power system meets its designers' primary goals - reliability and ease of operation. The redundancy and reliability of the 777's electrical systems were yet another contributor to ETOPS out-of-the-box approval.

Under normal circumstances, the electrical power system operates as two independent power channels, left and right. Electrical power busses may get power from different sources, and from each other. Power source selection depends on which power source is available, the operating phase of the air-

The extended Ram Air Turbine (RAT) is a source of emergency electrical power. Driven by two 42-inch diameter blades, the turbine powers a generator in the center and a hydraulic pump at the aft end of the assembly. (Boeing)

Two air-driven hydraulic pumps are located in the left wing-to-body fairing. Pneumatic air drive units are the large assemblies in the right of the photo. The smaller hydraulic pumps have braided hydraulic lines attached. (Boeing)

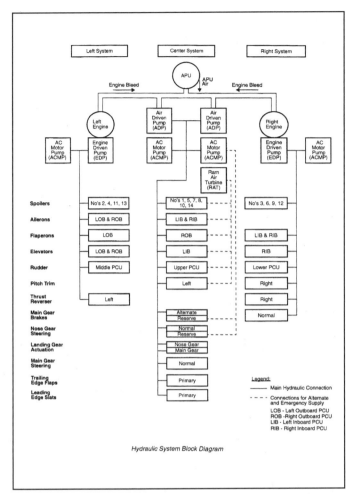

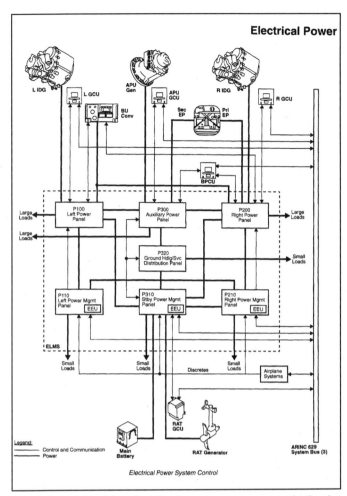

Block diagram of the 777 hydraulic system. There are three hydraulic systems for redundancy: the left system, center, and right systems. Each system has multiple pumps. (Boeing)

Block diagram of the electrical power system control. Like the hydraulic system, the electrical power system has three generators for redundancy. Two are engine driven Integrated Drive Generators, (IDG's) and the third is the APU generator. (Boeing)

craft, and the switching selected on the cockpit control panel. Power sources include ground, the left and right 120 kVA Integrated Drive Generators (IDGs) on the left and right engines, and the left and right backup generators with their permanent magnet generators located on each engine gear box. The 120 kVA generator mounted on the APU gearbox can supply power to all busses, on the ground or in flight.

Fuel tank locations in the 777-200 IGW. The -200 has a smaller center tank than the -200 Increased Gross Weight (IGW) or -300. Total fuel capacity for the -200 is 209,000 pounds, compared to 302,000 pounds for the -200 IGW and the -300. (Boeing)

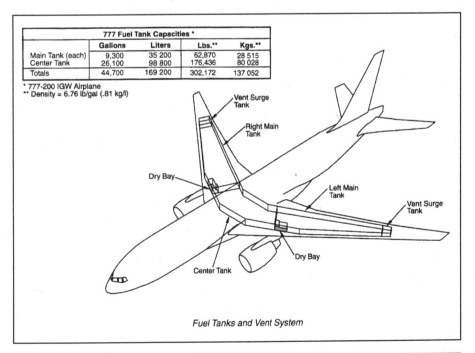

777 Fuel Tank Capacities *				
	Gallons	Liters	Lbs.**	Kgs.**
Main Tank (each)	9,300	35 200	62,870	28 515
Center Tank	26,100	98 800	176,436	80 028
Totals	44,700	169 200	302,172	137 052

* 777-200 IGW Airplane
** Density = 6.76 lb/gal (.81 kg/l)

Fuel Tanks and Vent System

When the APU starts, it automatically supplies power to the aircraft.

The backup generator system, a new feature, was built to support the ETOPS mission. It includes two variable-speed, variable-frequency generators, and a frequency converter supplying 400 Hz AC. In addition, the backup generators contain the permanent magnet generators that are the primary power sources for DC power to the flight controls.

The Electrical Load Management System (ELMS) is also new. This microprocessor-based load management system distributes, controls, and monitors loads on the aircraft, replacing most of the complex relay logic and circuit cards used in previous Boeing aircraft. This software-based control and monitoring logic system can be loaded from the maintenance access terminal, allowing easy upgrades to the system.

FUEL SYSTEM

The 777's fuel system combines the best of features in service on other

Fueling from a standard fuel truck under the right wing during a fit check demonstration on WA004 at Seatac Airport. The right wing refueling station is an option in addition to the left wing station. Both left and right stations can be used at the same time, offering faster refueling times. (Boeing/Brett Olson)

Fueling from a hydrant fuel truck, which provides the connection between the underground fuel system and the aircraft. The main difference between the hydrant fuel truck and the standard fuel truck is that the hydrant truck carries no fuel. (Boeing/Brett Olson)

Boeing airliners with newly designed features. It is the first production jetliner to use ultrasonic technology for measuring the amount of fuel in the tanks.

The Fuel Quantity Indicating System (FQIS) uses ultrasonic sensors to gauge fuel density and volume. These figures are used to calculate the quantity of fuel in the tank: that figure is then displayed on the Engine Indication and Crew Alerting System (EICAS) display in the Flight Station. The FQIS controls other functions, including an automatic refueling feature for specifying the amount of fuel needed. Refueling, done through the Integrated Refuel Panel (IRP), is automatically stopped when the specified load is reached.

Refueling and defueling are accomplished from the left wing refueling station located outboard of the engine, on the bottom of the wing. The IRP has two refuel adapters and a con-

The unique three-axle six-wheeled main landing gear on the 777. The landing gear truck is tilted up 13 degrees when extended in flight and moved to a five degree down position for retraction. (Boeing)

BOEING
777

trol panel - an additional right wing refueling station is optional. The -200 can be fully fueled in about 25 minutes with four refueling adapters. The IRP gives users the ability to refuel either by selecting loads for individual tanks, or using total fuel requirements.

The 777 has left, center, and main fuel tanks, with surge tanks outboard of each main tank. The-200 has a dry bay in the center tank where the wing passes through the fuselage. Both the -200 Increased Gross Weight (IGW) and the -300 carry fuel in the center tank. Total capacity for the -200 with the dry bay is 31,000 gallons. This figure increases to 45,220 gallons for the -200 IGW and -300. There are fifty-two ultrasonic fuel probes (made by Smith Industries) in the -200, and sixty probes in the -200 IGW and -300. Two AC powered fuel boost pumps in each of the three tanks supply fuel to the engines (two pumps in each tank provide redundant operation). A boost pump bypass valve in each tank allows the engines to suction feed fuel from either or both main tanks. Water scavenge pumps automatically remove water from low points in the tanks.

The fuel jettison system allows the pilots to dump fuel until the aircraft reaches maximum landing weight. This can be done automatically, if the system is armed. The Engine Indication and Crew Alerting System displays show fuel temperature, minimum allowable fuel temperature, fuel in each tank, and other fuel system information, including valve positions. They also display the maximum landing weight fuel load and the jettison time to reach this load. When all pumps and nozzles are operating, the jettison system can remove 280,000 pounds of fuel per hour.

From a maintenance standpoint, most of the fuel feed line replaceable units can be accessed from outside the fuel tank without draining or purging the fuel tanks. This is a major time-saver for fuel system maintenance.

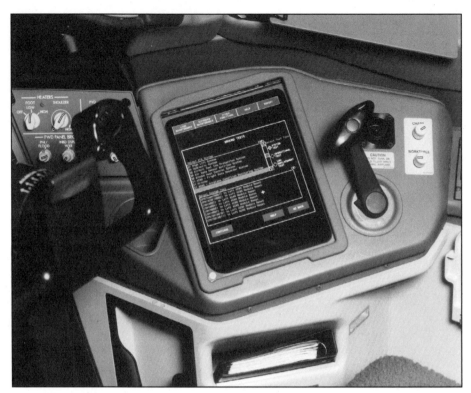

The steering tiller, located to the right of the first officer's optional side display, is one of the flight deck steering controls for taxiing on the ground. The captain's tiller is on the left outboard side of the flight deck. The tiller is in addition to the rudder pedals for steering on the ground. (Boeing)

LANDING GEAR SYSTEM

The 777 can be easily identified by its unique landing gear, when visible. Each main landing gear truck has three axles and six wheels. The nose landing gear has two wheels. This configuration effectively distributes pavement loading with no more than three landing gear struts. The main landing gear retracts inward, toward the center of the aircraft. The nose gear retracts forward.

The landing gear truck has two commanded tilt positions; front end thirteen degrees up from horizontal when landing gear is extended in flight, and truck tilted five degrees down for retraction to the stowed position in the wheel well. The truck positioner uses hydraulic pressure to put the truck in the 13-degree up or 5-degree down position. When the aircraft is on the ground, the landing gear is horizontal and aircraft weight overcomes the actuator force. Aircraft steering on the ground is accomplished through two controls in the flight deck:

the rudder pedals and steering tiller. The steering tiller is located on the outboard side of the captain's and first officer's stations. On the ground, the tiller is used for steering when inputs larger than those obtainable with full rudder pedal are required.

When using the tiller, the rear wheels of the six-wheel landing gear are steerable up to eight degrees left or right of center. When the nose gear turns to its maximum steered angle of seventy degrees the aft main wheels are at eight degrees. Aft wheels on the main landing gear are turned using an electrically commanded hydraulic actuator. They are locked in the centerline position when the pilot is using only the rudder pedals for steering, as he would for takeoff and landing.

A wheel-shaped handle, located on the flight deck, controls gear extension. This handle, which has UP and DOWN positions, lacks the OFF position other aircraft use to remove hydraulic pressure from the gear when

it is stowed. The 777 accomplishes the OFF function automatically through electrical control of the landing gear actuation system.

Backup alternate gear extension is controlled by a guarded toggle switch adjacent to the landing gear control handle. When this toggle switch is actuated, a dedicated alternate-extension powerpack pressurizes the hydraulic alternate-extension system. Landing gear doors are released and the landing gear is unlocked. Airloads pushing the landing gear down, combined with the landing gear's weight, will cause it to extend.

A tailstrike detection system lets the flight deck crew know if the aft fuselage of the aircraft strikes the runway due to over rotation on takeoff or landing. A sensor picks up the contact and displays a "TAIL STRIKE" message on the EICAS display. On the -300's longer length fuselage, a tailskid assembly has been added. The tailskid is hydraulically extended and retracted at the same time as landing gear extension and retraction. A collapsible cartridge is used to absorb the impact of a tailstrike.

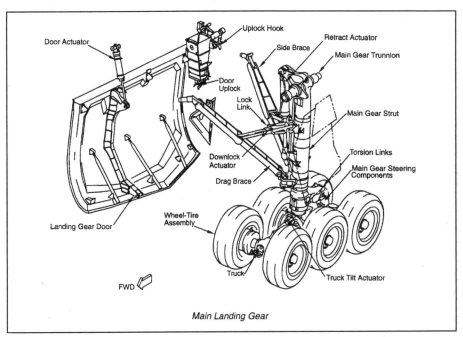

Main Landing Gear

Details of the 777's main landing gear. The landing gear door closes to reduce drag after the landing gear has been extended. It is reopened for retraction. (Boeing)

The brake system uses hydraulically actuated carbon brakes on all twelve wheels. Three hydraulic pressure sources provide redundancy for the system. Brakes can be applied using the pedals, or automatically through the autobrake system. The autobrake system, which can be used on landing, has five flight-station selectable levels ranging from mild to severe. This function is automatically disconnected when the brake pedals are used, much like the cruise control on your car.

Carbon brake wear is significantly affected by the number of times the brake is applied. Since all six brakes are not required during taxi, the taxi brake release system applies pressure to four of the six wheels on each landing gear. This reduces wear. Successive applications switch to the next set of four wheels to obtain an even distribution of brakes during the less demanding taxi phase.

Three indicator lights, located between the taxi and landing lights on the front of the nose landing gear, aid ground maintenance crews. Red BRAKE-ON light indicates pressure on left and right gear, amber PARKING BRAKE SET light indicates parking brake system is properly set, and blue BRAKE-OFF light indicates all brake pedals are released.

FLIGHT CONTROLS

External and flight deck flight controls appear standard; however, the

Wing high-lift surfaces of the flight control system. The Flap Slat Electronics Unit (FSEU) computer processes the high lift commands to the high lift surfaces of this fly-by-wire system. (Boeing)

Flight deck features color flat panel liquid crystal displays for the two pilot crew. Electronic checklists increase pilot efficiency. (Boeing)

totally electronically-controlled Primary Flight Controls are a first for a Boeing commercial aircraft. Two separate systems control the aircraft: the Primary Flight Control System (PFCS), and the High Lift Control System (HLCS). The PFCS supplies roll, pitch, and yaw control through ailerons, flaperons, spoilers, elevators, rudder, and a horizontal stabilizer. HLCS controls the inboard and outboard trailing edge flaps, the leading edge slats, and the Kruger flaps.

A major difference between conventional mechanical primary flight controls and fly-by-wire flight controls lies in the connection between the flight deck and actuator at the control surface. In the conventional control system, mechanical cables run from the control column or rudder pedals directly to the actuator at the control surface. In the fly-by-wire or electronic flight control system, electric wires have replaced mechanical connections. A signal is sent from the transducer, located at the flight column, to the flight computer. The flight computer processes the signal before sending it to the actuator; consequently, the actuator is now electronically controlled.

There are several advantages to the electronic flight control system. The conventional cable-controlled system has a weight penalty because of long cable runs, which add the weight of pulleys and support brackets. A cable-controlled system is also harder to maintain. Cable tensions change and need to be adjusted; pulleys and cables need to be lubricated. The electronic flight control system lets components like the yaw damper be eliminated because these functions are handled electronically, using existing actuators in the electronic flight control system. Additionally, an electronic system is able to react more quickly than even an alert pilot can. This allows the design of smaller control surfaces, further reducing weight. Control laws are part of the operating system of the flight control computer and can be modified to a certain extent by software. This provides flexibility for updating a flight control system.

An electronic flight control system retains the good features of a mechanically controlled system, eliminating the bad ones. Added protections and

features include turn compensation, bank angle protection, pitch control and stability augmentation, stall and overspeed protection, and thrust asymmetry compensation, used (for example) when an engine is lost. All of these items have been incorporated into the 777's electronic flight control system. They don't limit the action of a pilot - they deter the pilot from exceeding a limit.

In keeping with the company's design philosophy for the flight control system, Boeing maintained system operations that would be familiar to the pilot and consistent with pilot training. The 777 uses a yoke in the cockpit, for example, not a side stick controller.

Even though electronic flight control systems do not have any feel, feel forces were maintained to give the pilot the type of cues he would get from a conventional mechanical flight control system. An example of this is the gradient control actuator, which is attached to the control column. This component proportionally increases the amount of column force the pilot feels when pushing the yoke to a higher airspeed. During autopilot operation, backdrive actuators move the control column and wheel and rudder pedals in response to autopilot commands, providing the pilot with visual feedback of autopilot output.

The Primary Flight Control System has three operating modes: Normal, Secondary, and Direct. In the Normal mode, the Primary Flight Computer (PFC) supplies all commands to the Actuator Control Electronics (ACE) at the control surface. This mode provides full functionality. All enhanced performance, envelope protection, and ride quality features are included.

Operation in the Secondary mode is very similar to the primary mode, although system functionality is reduced. Envelope protection functions, for example, may not be active in the secondary mode. The PFC automatically transfers from the primary to the secondary mode after sufficient failures in the system, or interfacing systems, prevent Normal mode operation.

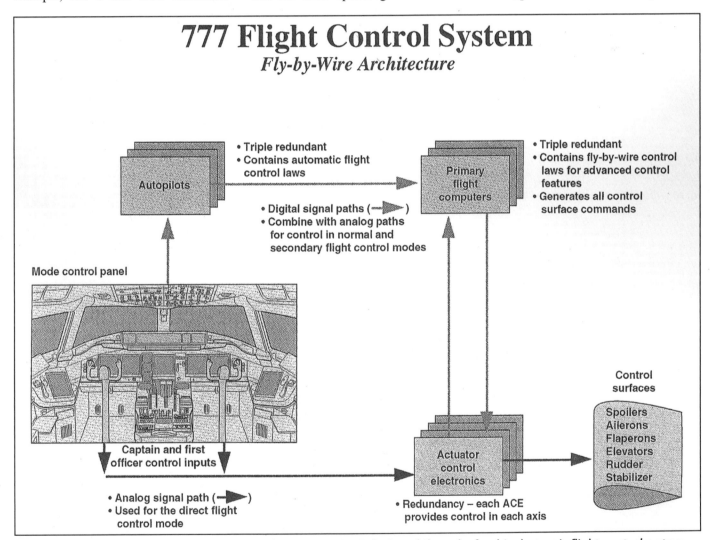

777 Flight Control System
Fly-by-Wire Architecture

Fly-by-wire flight control system architecture diagram. Boeing's design philosophy for this electronic flight control system maintains the pilot cues that would come from a conventional mechanical flight control system, even though electronic flight control systems do not have any feel to them. This includes keeping a yoke rather than a side stick controller in the cockpit. (Boeing)

A good photo showing the flaps and leading edge slats deployed to the high lift position with the aircraft in slow flight and the landing gear down. The High Lift Control System (HLCS), an electronic fly-by-wire system, has inboard and outboard trailing edge flaps, leading edge slats, and Krueger flaps. (Boeing/Jeff Rumsey)

In Direct mode, the PFC is removed from the loop. Pilot commands go directly from pilot controller transducers to the actuator controller electronics. This mode can be activated manually, by pilot activation of the PFC Disconnect Switch, or automatically, on failure of the PFC, internal ACE failures, or loss of the flight control's data busses. In the Direct mode, aircraft handling characteristics closely match those of the Secondary mode.

A cable-driven system controls two spoilers (numbers four and eleven) and the stabilizer. This alternate horizontal stabilizer control is accomplished by using two pitch trim levers on the control stand in the cockpit. Spoiler panels four and eleven also serve as speed brakes, deflecting to forty-five degrees. Once the spoilers have been extended by a speed brake command, control wheel (Roll) to speed brake command

mixing is no longer available.

Even before the first flight a significant amount of testing occurred on the flight control system. Individual components were tested in various labs, at the manufacturers, and in the System Integration Lab (SIL), which put all of the individual Primary Flight Control System components together for yet more rigorous testing. Flight control software was tested on flight simulators and a Boeing 757 Flying Test Bed to evaluate the operation and performance of the 777 fly-by-wire flight control laws in flight.

A lot of redundancy was designed into the 777's flight control system: electrical power sources, hydraulic power sources, electronics, and alternate operation modes included. All of the flight control features contributed to flight safety and ETOPS out of the box reliability.

FLIGHT DECK

The aircraft has a two-pilot flight deck with room for two observers. It has the latest in flat panel Liquid Crystal Display (LCD) technology, along with the digital flight deck technology already proven on the 757, 767, and 747-400. Many flight crew operations that were performed manually will now be accomplished automatically, reducing workload.

The flight deck design used input from the customer airlines to an extent unparalleled in aviation history: a part of the Working Together philosophy adapted by the design team. Eleven of the initial customer airlines participated in three dedicated flight deck design reviews during the initial design process. Pilots and representatives from each of the airlines spent two-and-a-half days in the engineering simulator, evaluating the flight deck

Illustration of the flight control systems on the 777. Kruger flaps are on the bottom of the wing. They seal the gap between the engine strut and the inboard slat. (Boeing)

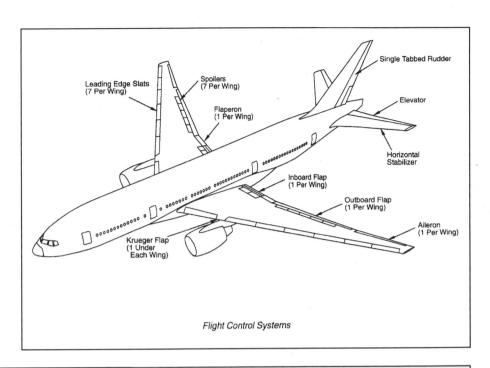

Flight Control Systems

Leading Edge Slats (7 Per Wing)
Spoilers (7 Per Wing)
Single Tabbed Rudder
Flaperon (1 Per Wing)
Elevator
Horizontal Stabilizer
Inboard Flap (1 Per Wing)
Outboard Flap (1 Per Wing)
Aileron (1 Per Wing)
Krueger Flap (1 Under Each Wing)

Flight deck layout shows efficient use of space and attention to detail for pilot comfort items. Notice the two observer seats in addition to the captain's and first officer's seats. (Boeing)

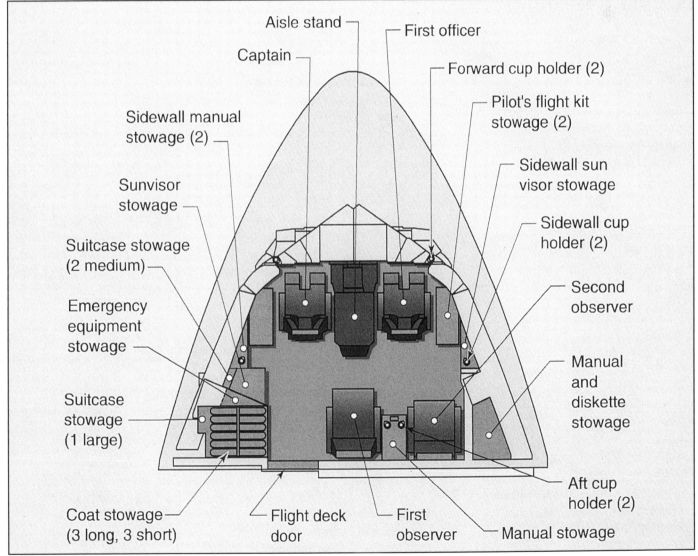

Aisle stand
Captain
First officer
Forward cup holder (2)
Pilot's flight kit stowage (2)
Sidewall manual stowage (2)
Sunvisor stowage
Sidewall sun visor stowage
Sidewall cup holder (2)
Suitcase stowage (2 medium)
Second observer
Emergency equipment stowage
Manual and diskette stowage
Suitcase stowage (1 large)
Aft cup holder (2)
Coat stowage (3 long, 3 short)
Flight deck door
First observer
Manual stowage

A United 777 take-off from Los Angeles with landing gear doors almost closed. Closing the doors once the landing gear is extended reduces drag until it is time to retract the gear. (Stephen Griffin)

design. The 777 used the 747-400 flight deck arrangement and 767/757 system interfaces as its basis, resulting in a high degree of operational commonality - a benefit to pilots and airlines transitioning between various or multiple aircraft equipment types.

Using flat-panel LCDs in place of earlier mechanical instruments or cathode ray tubes (CRTs), the 777 has a "glass cockpit". Flat-panel LCDs have many advantages over CRTs. They save weight, use less space, and generate less heat while providing greater reliability and a longer service life. Their lower power requirements mean that five main flight displays can be operated on standby power. Additionally LCDs, with a larger useable screen, are easier to read and have better visibility over a wide range of flight deck lighting, from night to bright sunlight.

The basic layout in the flight deck uses six large LCDs, with five in a row across the cockpit. Two Primary Flight Displays (PFDs) are located at the captain's and first officer's outboard panel positions. Two Inboard Multifunction Displays (MFDs), are normally used to display navigation data. The center forward panel has the standby instruments

on the left and the EICAS display in the center. Below, in the forward aisle stand panel, are the lower center MFD unit and the three flight management Control Display Units (CDUs) that control what is presented on the captain's and first officer's MFDs.

Any of the three MFDs can display the following information, as selected with the push of a button on the glareshield Display Select Panel: navigation display, secondary engine indications (like oil pressure), status display, electronic checklist, system synoptics (electrical system, hydraulic system, fuel system etc.), and communications (integrated data link). Additional information control on a specific display can be programmed using the CDU or cursor control devices. CDUs provide data presentation and entry capabilities for flight management functions. They are the primary interface with the integrated Airplane Information Management Systems (AIMS).

The Maintenance Access Terminal (MAT) is located at the second observer's position behind the first officer. Through MAT, the maintenance crew can request system and component fault and maintenance information,

conduct airplane systems and components ground tests, and load software into components that need on-board software loads. Since the maintenance crew no longer needs to use controls and displays in the flight station, busy pre-flight activities can go on simultaneously, without interfering with one another. The MAT is also available as a portable unit that can hook up at five different locations on the aircraft.

AIRPLANE INFORMATION MANAGEMENT SYSTEM (AIMS)

Large amounts of information are required from almost all of the 777's aircraft systems. The 777 AIMS computer system is behind a number of avionics systems on the aircraft, including the primary display, the aircraft condition monitoring, flight management computing, thrust management computing, data communications, the flight data recorder, and the central maintenance computing system. AIMS integrates avionic computing functions that require large amounts of data collection, processing, and calculations.

In the flight station, AIMS provides the majority of the flight crew interface. AIMS controls and displays

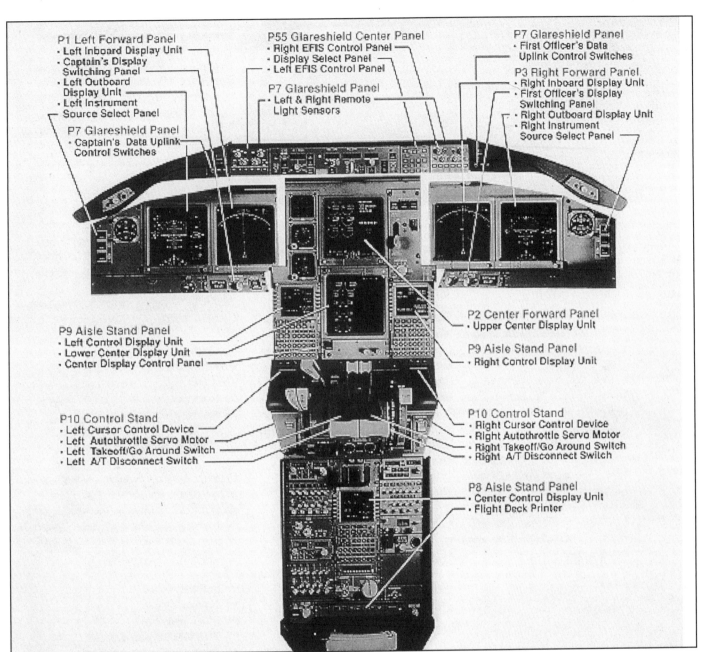

Location and identification photo of the major pilot interface elements in the cockpit. The systems are well integrated through the Airplane Information Management System (AIMS). (Boeing)

information on the cockpit's six LCDs. This includes navigation data, airplane status, flight plan data, engine indicating and crew alerting data, maintenance page data, communications data, and electronic checklists. Airplane status covers dispatch status as well as APU, oxygen, and hydraulic information. Graphical presentations of systems status, called "synoptic displays", show schematic-type presentations with actual paths and positions of valves and switches. Systems using the synoptic format include landing gear, fuel, doors, flight controls, hydraulic, electrical, and environmental control. The three CDUs, the DSP, the two EFIS (Electronic Flight Instrument System), the control panels, the two display switching panels, and the two cursor control devices are all AIMS flight station interface devices.

The cursor control devices, located on the center control stand outboard of the throttles, are a new feature. A hand/palm support and touch-sensitive pad responds to finger movement. A select switch on the side of the cursor control is pressed to activate the selection when the cursor is in the desired position. The cursor control device is used to control menus, point and select items on the MFD, point and select items on the side displays, and manage communications.

AIMS has two cabinets located in the main equipment center. Each cabinet has eight line-replaceable modules. Four are input-output modules and

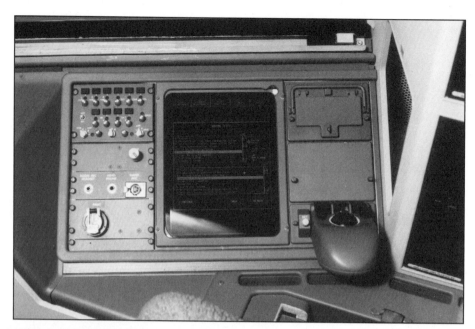

Maintenance Access Terminal (MAT), used for ground crew troubleshooting, is located behind the first officer. At this station, a mechanic or technician can obtain fault and maintenance information and run ground tests. New software may also be loaded at this terminal. (Boeing)

four are core processor modules. The cabinets, which operate as the main computer for several avionic systems, interface with approximately 130 LRUs, sensors, switches, and indicators. This large number of interfaces makes it possible for AIMS to integrate information gathered from a majority of aircraft systems into one place.

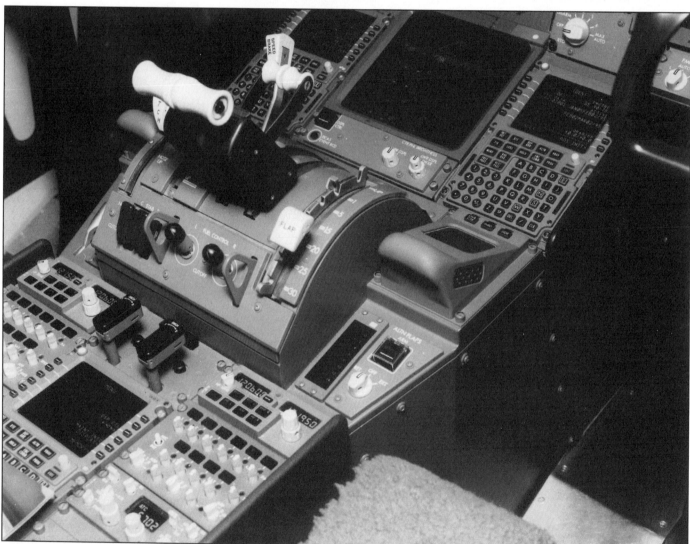

Part of the Airplane Information Management System, the touch pad cursor control device is located to the right of the flap handle. This device is similar to a "mouse" on a personal computer. The palm rest provides a steady support for the pilot's hand, in bumpy air. (Boeing)

FLIGHT TEST AND CERTIFICATION

The Boeing 777 underwent the most comprehensive test program in aviation history, a statement that does not just refer to the ten aircraft in the flight test program, but also includes all testing done at the suppliers and in over fifty-four labs and test facilities at Boeing. This extensive testing was absolutely essential since one of the requirements was to have to have a service ready aircraft which could fly ETOPS routes upon introduction to service on a date five years into the future.

SIL

Systems Integration Lab (SIL) testing started thirteen months before first flight. It was a major tool in accomplishing many tasks prior to flight test. Bob Dawes, then Test Manager of the SIL and currently Chief Engineer for the 737 test program, described the mission statement of the SIL, as follows. "The purpose of testing in the 777 Systems Integration Lab was to validate correct performance of electrical/electronic systems interfaces (physical and functional) during concurrent multiple system operation,

Systems Integration Lab (SIL) was so complete, it was often referred to as "airplane zero". Here Capt. John Cashman, chief pilot (center), prepares for a "takeoff". SIL testing started 13 months before the first flight of the 777. (Boeing)

Wing tip of the 777 static test airframe is deflected 24 feet before breaking in a wing destruct test. This test provides data for growth capabilities of the wings by loading them beyond their design ultimate load requirement. (Boeing)

GE90-85B ready for testing at the wind tunnel test site at the GE Aircraft Engines test complex near Peebles, Ohio. Engine development testing starts a long time before the first flight of a new aircraft. (GE Aircraft Engines)

including failure modes. Testing was performed in a laboratory airplane environment prior to integration on the airplane. The SIL supported the 777 Flight Test Program and was also used to support manufacturing and customer services test requirements, including validation of functional test procedures, Automated Test Equipment (ATE), and maintenance manual system test/troubleshooting procedures and maintenance tools."

Testing started at the supplier, with verification of the individual components. Functional organizations included electrical, avionics, propulsion, payload, flight control, mechanical, hydraulic, flight deck, and environmental systems. After supplier verification, the "components" went through

GE90-85B engine with the cowl open on the 747 flying test bed at Mojave California. Technician standing at the aft end of the engine makes a good size comparison. (GE Aircraft Engines)

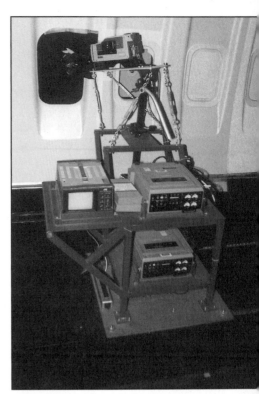

Instrumentation video camera installation in the forward cabin area of the GE 747 flying testbed. The camera covers the inlet end of the test engine. This view is recorded and displayed, in real time, to the test pilot. (Author)

GE90-85B flight test engine mounted on the 747 flying testbed at Mojave California. Notice the ground clearance on this enormous engine. (GE Aircraft Engines)

validation, by functional organization, in stand-alone test labs and sub-system integration facilities (fifty-four labs of this type were used during the 777 program). This phase of the validation program ensured that each system performed as intended.

Major integration laboratories included an electrical power systems lab, the flight deck simulator, and the flight controls test rig. The electrical power systems lab brought the electrical system components together, including the generators, control systems, and the distribution system. A flight deck simulator brought together a large portion of the aircraft's electronics and supplied a realistic pilot interface, including a visual system. The flight controls test rig, called the "Iron Bird" because of its massive steel framework, integrated the fly-by-wire flight control system with hydraulic pumps, actuators, and tubing. The test rig used real and simulated flight control surfaces. A flight deck allowed pilot-in-the-loop testing.

Following successful testing in the stand-alone test facilities, all components were assembled for airplane-level validation in the SIL. The collection of components was so complete that the SIL was referred to as Flight Test Airplane "0". The SIL had 900 of the 1200 factory production wire bundles. The fact that these bundles were built by the production shop using production drawings allowed early resolution of any problems in producibility and functionality. In fact, 110 problems were uncovered in time to correct them for incorporation into the first aircraft.

Engine flight testing of a GE90-85B engine, mounted at the inboard location on the left wing of GE's 747 flying testbed. The data collection system on board the test bed has the capability to record 3000 measurements. Typical crew size during test flights ranges from 16 to 25. (GE Aircraft Engines)

Cockpit of the GE 747 flying testbed. Note the video display monitor on the top center of the glareshield. This provides a real time display of what is happening at the inlet of the engine. (Author)

AIRLINER**TECH**
SERIES

An air-cooled resistance type load bank is mounted on the bottom of the left wing of the GE flying testbed. The load bank is used for applying electrical loads to the test engine generator. (Author)

Over 100 real airplane Line Replace-able Units (LRUs), such as flight computers and electrical inverters, were installed in "Airplane 0".

"The Systems Integration Lab was essentially a full aircraft flown by flight test pilots," said Dawes. The only items missing were rows of seats and the aircraft's outer skin. Harris Nighthawk computers, which simulate air speed, altitude, temperature, runway, and navigation environment, were used to provide a flight world environment. Systems performance and interactions were recorded by a data acquisition system with 61,000 data channels.

A total of 1,544 piloted flight hours and 4,238 ground test hours were accomplished during SIL testing. Aircraft level validation categories included production functional test, production flight test, maintenance, routine aircraft operation, non-routine aircraft operation, operation with failures, relevant experience, and other categories. Tests were run using cards and proce-

dures essentially identical to those used during the actual flight test. This process allowed Boeing engineers to find and correct problems that otherwise would not have been discovered until the aircraft was either assembled or undergoing ground and flight tests. It saved considerable time and money, and protected the program from costly delay.

STRUCTURAL TESTING

Full-scale static and fatigue structural tests were started early in the development program: the second 777 off the assembly line provided the static test airframe. Full-scale static and fatigue structural tests exposed two complete airframes to design and operating loads in order to meet certification requirements for the FAA/JAA, and to validate structural analysis methods. Design limit load was defined as the highest possible loading under extreme flight or ground conditions that an airframe would ever experience in the life of the 777 fleet,

as defined by regulatory or Boeing-specified requirements.

Static Testing

The static test aircraft was structurally complete, although it lacked payload and systems. The aircraft was positioned on a structural slab with a system of towers and reaction fixtures, which supported hydraulic actuators that applied loads to the test aircraft. Loads were gradually increased to one hundred percent of the test load in twenty-percent increments.

The major portion of static testing occurred at the same time as the flight test program, which provided an opportunity to compare actual flight loads to static test loads. Flight test aircraft were limited to a temporary operating envelope of eighty percent of design limit loads during initial flight-testing. This limitation was removed after certain static tests successfully proved the structure could withstand design limit loads.

Static testing culminated in the wing destruct test, which took place on Jan. 4, 1995. This test, developed by Boeing, explored the growth capabilities of the wings by loading them beyond their design ultimate load requirement. Design ultimate load is defined as typically equal to limit loads multiplied by a safety factor of 1.5. In other words, ultimate load is 150 percent of limit load. Each wing was loaded to 103 percent of ultimate load, at which point both wings failed almost simultaneously. The largest measured wing tip deflection was more than 24 feet!

Fatigue Testing

Full-scale fatigue tests exposed a structurally complete 777 airframe to common operating loads. The primary benefit of fatigue tests is to lead the fleet in locating areas of the aircraft that might exhibit early fatigue problems. Each flight cycle represented a ground-air-ground flight profile that included ground handling, taxi-out, takeoff, cabin pressurization, cruise, depressurization, descent, buffeting, landing, and taxi-in.

Flight cycle loads were applied an average of every four minutes, twenty-four hours a day, which explains how two aircraft lifetimes could be simulated in less than a year. To illustrate how quickly a flight profile was accomplished in the fatigue test, the pressurization-to-cruise altitude was done in fifteen seconds with two 1500-horsepower compressors that pumped air into the fuselage through sixty-two modified passenger windows.

FLYING TEST BEDS

Flying Test Beds (FTBs) played an important part in the development of the 777. FTBs are usually developed aircraft that are modified to carry the components or systems of a new aircraft, like the 777, to obtain development data in the real flight world. This is accomplished early in the schedule so design changes can be incorporated into the new aircraft prior to first flight.

Three major FTBs were used in the development phase. The Fly-By-Wire (FBW) flight control system received early testing and development on a modified Boeing 757. General Electric did a considerable amount of testing on its new GE90 engine with its 747 flying test bed. Boeing operated another 747 FTB for testing the Pratt & Whitney 4084 engine and the Rolls Royce Trent 800 engines.

FBW

Boeing modified a production 757-200 (NB143) to emulate the 777 FBW control laws, in order to evaluate the operation and performance of these control laws in flight. The conventional 757 longitudinal flight control system was retained but controlled by only the captain's column. The pilot evaluated the FBW system in the first officer's seat, while the safety pilot function was conducted from the captain's seat.

To evaluate the longitudinal system, the first officer's control column drove the existing 757 left and right autopilots (flight control computers), which were modified to operate like

Pratt & Whitney's PW4084 engine in checkout. This checkout occurs at the Pratt & Whitney factory long before the engine flies on the testbed or the 777. (Pratt & Whitney)

Boeing's 747 flying testbed takes off with Pratt & Whitney's PW4084 mounted on the left inboard pylon. A total of seventeen flights and 56 hours were flown with the P&W engine on the Boeing 747 flying test bed. (Pratt & Whitney)

Rolls-Royce Trent 800 engine during start tests on the Boeing 747 flying testbed. Ground and flight tests were accomplished on the Boeing 747 operating out of Boeing Field in Seattle Washington. (Boeing/Jim Niswonger)

Flight test water ballast system in the 777 consists of 48 barrels that are used for changing weight and center-of-gravity during testing. 24 barrels are located in the front end of the aircraft and 24 in the aft, so water can be pumped back and forth through the pipes to change the center of gravity. (Boeing)

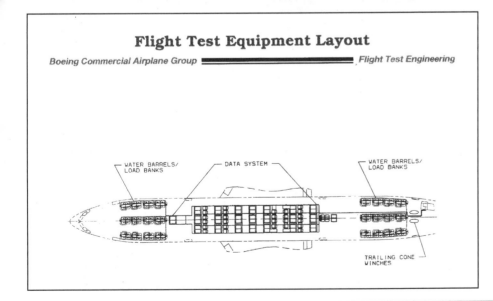

Flight Test Equipment Layout

Boeing Commercial Airplane Group ━━━━━━━━━ Flight Test Engineering

WATER BARRELS/ LOAD BANKS   DATA SYSTEM   WATER BARRELS/ LOAD BANKS

TRAILING CONE WINCHES

Flight test equipment layout drawing showing water ballast and data system locations. The static pressure trailing cone winches are located aft of the water ballast system. (Boeing)

FBW computers. These computers emulated the -200 FBW control laws and drove their respective autopilot actuators to control the aircraft pitch axis. Directional control laws were emulated in the existing 757 yaw dampers, with corresponding modifications to the normal 757 directional system.

A flight test instrumentation and data system was also installed in the 757. This system consisted of an instrumentation measurement acquisition system, an airborne monitoring system (for real-time in-flight monitoring) and a telemetry monitoring system (for transmitting the data to a ground station during minimum crew flights). The program was planned as a 250 flight-hour program. 1500 measurements were recorded and analyzed.

The control law portion of the 757 FBW Flying Test Bed program involved system-level test maneuvers for optimization of control laws and integrated

Instrumentation cameras located on the bottom of the fuselage of WA001. These cameras were used during the rejected takeoff tests at Edwards Air Force Base, California. (Boeing/ Brett Olson)

system-test maneuvers to verify desirable handling qualities. Desirable features were retained: undesirable features refined, changed, or modified. Three Boeing pilots were used in the initial structured testing. After the system was refined, additional pilots participated in a validation test phase to confirm the Fly-By-Wire configurations established by the original three pilots.

Pratt & Whitney PW4084 Engine FTB

The Pratt & Whitney PW4084 engine was operated on a Boeing-leased 747 to demonstrate engine operability throughout the intended flight envelope. A key objective of this FTB flight test was to demonstrate engine/inlet com-

Instrumentation trailing static cone hanging from tip of the rudder with the body trailing cone line just aft of the APU exhaust port. A microphone on a pole near the APU exhaust is for noise measurement testing at Glasgow, Montana. (Boeing/Joe Parke)

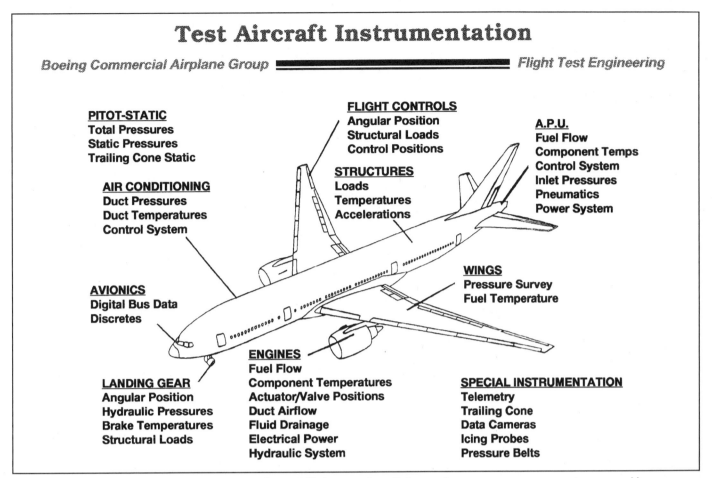

Test Aircraft Instrumentation

PITOT-STATIC
Total Pressures
Static Pressures
Trailing Cone Static

AIR CONDITIONING
Duct Pressures
Duct Temperatures
Control System

AVIONICS
Digital Bus Data
Discretes

LANDING GEAR
Angular Position
Hydraulic Pressures
Brake Temperatures
Structural Loads

FLIGHT CONTROLS
Angular Position
Structural Loads
Control Positions

STRUCTURES
Loads
Temperatures
Accelerations

ENGINES
Fuel Flow
Component Temperatures
Actuator/Valve Positions
Duct Airflow
Fluid Drainage
Electrical Power
Hydraulic System

A.P.U.
Fuel Flow
Component Temps
Control System
Inlet Pressures
Pneumatics
Power System

WINGS
Pressure Survey
Fuel Temperature

SPECIAL INSTRUMENTATION
Telemetry
Trailing Cone
Data Cameras
Icing Probes
Pressure Belts

Types of instrumentation measurements on the 777 flight test aircraft. Items shown are measurements grouped by category. Any one item may have many actual measurements. For instance, brake temperatures under landing gear may have fifty or more thermocouples to measure brake temperatures. (Boeing)

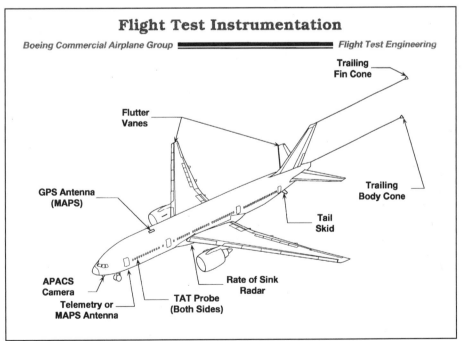

Flight Test Instrumentation

Trailing
Fin Cone

Flutter
Vanes

GPS Antenna
(MAPS)

Trailing
Body Cone

Tail
Skid

APACS
Camera

Rate of Sink
Radar

Telemetry or
MAPS Antenna

TAT Probe
(Both Sides)

Locations of external flight test instrumentation are illustrated. True Air Temperature, (TAT) probes are located on both sides of the forward fuselage. Metal plates with probes attached are installed in place of two passenger windows. (Boeing)

patibility and to confirm that fan blade stresses were within design limits. High inlet angle of attack causes inlet flow distortion and increased fan blade stress, and can also cause fan stall/engine stall; conditions that you don't want to encounter for the first time in flight, where both engines are the same type, as they would be on the 777 flight test. A dual engine stall could occur. This test needs to be done in the air - high angle of attack testing with the "G" loads that occur in flight cannot be done on the ground.

Systems-integration flight testing of the engine and airframe components was also of critical importance. Equipped with a Full Authority Digital Electronic Control (FADEC), the 777 engine uses the aircraft's high-speed ARINC 429 databus, also tested on the FTB. Electrical loads for testing the engine generators were created using both 80 kVA and 20 kVA water barrel load banks.

The first flight of the PW4084 engine on the FTB occurred on November 9, 1993 out of Boeing Field. Seventeen flights were flown for a total of fifty-six flight hours. Two successful take-offs were made with engine thrusts of 84,000 pounds and 74,000 pounds. Tests included steady state power calibrations, stall line mapping, accel/decel maneuvers, wind-mill relights, airstarts, nacelle component cooling during climb flight, aircraft maneuvers, and a thrust reverser taxi test.

GE90 Engine FTB

Aircraft engine testing starts a long time before the first flight of a new aircraft. Testing for the GE90 engine for the Boeing 777 began at the outdoor facility located in Peebles, Ohio. Following the completion of developmental and certification tests (which included performance and operability tests), the GE90 went on GE's 747 Flying Test Bed (FTB). On December 6, 1993, at Mojave California, General Electric flew the GE90 high bypass turbofan engine for the first time. GE's FTB has a complete on-board data collection system with the capability to record 3000 measurements (2000 digital and 1000 ARINC bus measurements). A typical flight test crew ranges between sixteen and twenty-five people.

GE's ability to conduct key flight tests as part of the overall engine test method has ensured a good balance between ground test, simulations, diagnostics, and the real-world operating environment. The testbed concept focuses on engine testing with ample data to understand the operating characteristics.

GE's current data system, permanently installed in the 747 FTB, can measure the equivalent of several test phases on one flight. This is an improvement over smaller systems, like GE's earlier 500 measurement system, which made testing in phases necessary. Different instrumentation had

Data systems in operation on the 777. Typical crew size during these flights ranges from 8 to 25. (Boeing)

to be installed for different tests, so downtime occurred when the aircraft was switched between phases. Although many of the test conditions for different phases were the same, as many as eight instrumentation phase changes had been made in the past due to limited data system capability. The current data system, which flies several phases at once, saves time and money.

"Another advantage to real time data on the FTB is engineers can walk off the aircraft at the end of a flight with the data they need in hand," said Philip Schultz, Chief Test Pilot for General Electric. "We need to be able to relate the data being taken to that of our ground test facilities. We need to be able to return to the same point in the sky, with the same conditions, on different flights. A key tool incorporated into the testbed in order to accomplish this task was the cockpit data display system."

Test engine conditions were becoming harder to set with the limited data available in the cockpit. The improved cockpit display system in GE's 747 FTB has proven extremely valuable in setting test conditions, providing real time data to engineering monitors, and capturing the data

required to understand unexpected test results. One of the cockpit displays is a video picture, in real time, of the front of the test engine. A video camera mounted in the cabin looks out the window down the engine inlet. This video picture is simultaneously recorded and displayed on a monitor on the top of the glareshield in the cockpit.

To test the generator operation on the GE90 in flight, an air-cooled electrical resistance load bank was mounted externally in a pod on the bottom of the left wing, at the existing spare engine hard point. The load bank, which is a basically a dummy load that can be applied or removed to fit a given test condition, applies various loads to the generator.

General Electric's 747 flying testbed made it possible for GE to conduct a full range of flight tests on the GE90 engines in a cost-efficient manner, that obtained real-time data, before the engines were installed on the 777. The converted Boeing 747 is serial number 16, a former Pan American Airways aircraft.

Rolls Royce Trent 800 Engine FTB

Similar testing was accomplished on the Rolls Royce Trent 800 engine using the same 747 FTB used in the

777 Program Schedule

777-200 Development/Certification Flight Test Plan

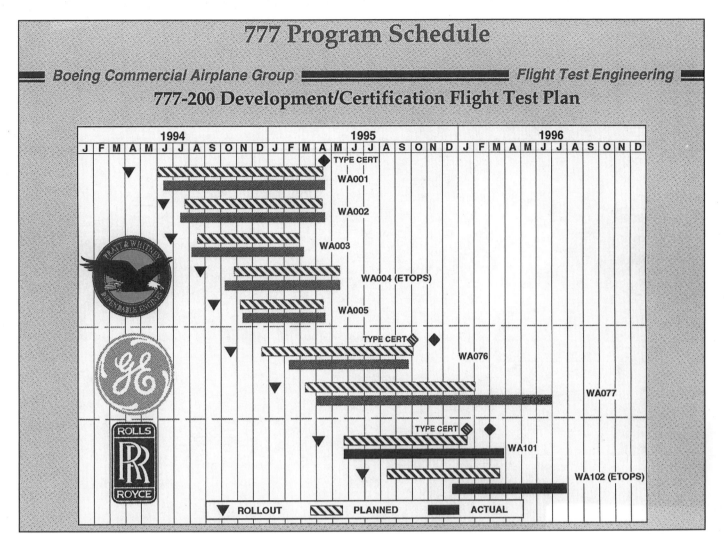

Flight test development and certification schedule shows time spans for the nine primary aircraft in the 777-200 flight test program. A total of 2,155 tests were accomplished using 10 flight test aircraft. (Boeing)

PW4084 tests. Boeing used RA001, the first 747 ever built, for these tests. RA001 is now in the Seattle Museum of Flight.

LAGOS

Boeing's LAGOS (Large Airplane Ground Operations Simulator) is a testbed, albeit not a flying testbed. This huge mobile simulator has a cockpit, nose landing gear, and main landing gear located in geometrical locations that correspond to the actual aircraft hardware. Although it looks like a huge piece of farm irrigation equipment, LAGOS played a very useful role in 777 development. The -300's 140-foot long wheelbase (the distance between the nose landing gear and the main landing gear) is longer than that of any

other airliner. The cockpit is located way out in front of the nose gear, which complicates the pilot's task of taxiing and maneuvering on taxi ways that might be as narrow as 150 feet wide.

LAGOS was used for pilot evaluations of the ground maneuvering capability of the -300, the stretched version of the 777. Pilots felt they needed additional visual cues for taxiing the longer aircraft (it has an 18-foot longer wheelbase than the -200) so three external video cameras were added.

INSTRUMENTATION

The aircraft instrumentation system must be designed, built, and installed before flight testing can start. This is no small task. 777 flight test aircraft interiors vary, and most are full of

test equipment rather than passenger seats and galleys.

The water ballast system, which consists of forty-eight barrels mounted on the cabin floor, manifolds together with plumbing lines and pumps. Water can be moved around to change the weight distribution, which in turn changes the Center of Gravity (CG) of the aircraft for various test conditions. Twenty-four barrels are located in the front end and twenty-four in the aft end of the cabin, allowing forward, aft, or any CG in between.

The airborne data system fills a major part of the aircraft's interior. There are consoles for data acquisition, recording, monitoring, analysis, and video stations. The video rack can record up to twelve cameras simultane-

Elaborate test fixtures are installed around the aircraft for instrumentation load calibration. Fixtures are used to support the actuators that apply the calibration loads to the aircraft. For instance, strain gages on the horizontal stabilizer would read the known loads applied by the actuator. This would be used to calibrate the strain gages. (Boeing/Jeff Rumsey)

ously, with distribution for on-board monitoring at the analysis stations. Various sensors throughout the aircraft feed data to the data acquisition and monitoring stations.

Jeff Goedhard, Test Director on the 777-300 WB501, explained the aircraft's dual trailing cones. "Trailing fin and trailing body cones are used to get a clean static pressure source for the flight test airspeed system. The trailing cone is normally retracted for take-off and then extended in flight. A powered large diameter reel in the aft end of the cabin is used to reel the cone in and out. The actual cone is a drag device to pull the static sensor out and is located just forward of the cone. The reason

for two trailing cones was to have an option on at least one source that was not in disturbed air during a particular flight test maneuver."

A flight test tail skid is used on the underside of the aircraft's fuselage. While conducting VMU (Velocity Minimum Unstick) speed testing, tail dragging usually occurs. An oak block is used as a wear attachment on the tail skid. Flutter vanes, electro-mechanical devices located on the tip of the right wing and on the tip of the right horizontal stabilizer, are an in-flight method of verifying that the aircraft is flutter-free through its normal operating range. The flutter vanes are driven at various frequencies to try to excite

the natural structural frequencies of the wing and stabilizer.

Rate of sink radar, located on the bottom of the fuselage, is used to obtain accurate sink rates for landing tests. True Air Temperature (TAT) probes are accurate instrumentation sensors located in plates that replace two of the windows. The telemetry antenna, also on the bottom of the fuselage, is used for transmitting flight data to the ground station during minimum crew tests. Minimum flight crew tests are conducted from the telemetry room where the ground based monitor system is located.

To give the reader a feel for the amount of instrumentation required on the 777 fight test program, the number

Number one 777 performs a taxi test prior to first flight. Taxi tests are used as part of the preflight checkout prior to a first flight. Usually accomplished several days before a first flight, taxi tests provide an opportunity to exercise many of the aircraft systems in a controlled environment that approaches take-off speeds. (Boeing)

Five Pratt & Whitney powered flight test 777-200s at Boeing Field, Seattle on February 15, 1997. WA001 through WA005 were the first five aircraft in flight test. (Boeing/Bob Carnahan)

of measurements recorded on the primary instrumented test aircraft are shown, as follow:

WA001 - 1904 analog measurements and 144 buses measured.

WA002 - 2112 analog measurements and 131 buses measured.

WA003 - 2530 analog measurements and 125 buses measured.

WA004 - Padds II data system for the ETOPS Service Ready testing.

WA005 - 413 analog measurements and 32 buses measured.

WA076 - 1245 analog measurements and 127 buses measured.

WA101 - 1240 analog measurements and 118 buses measured.

Instrumentation calibration is used to verify instrumentation values to known quantities. Elaborate test fixtures are installed around the aircraft for load calibrations. A metal framework, not unlike the structure used for the structural load tests, is built up. Hydraulic load actuators are used to apply known loads while the strain gages on the aircraft read out the loads.

777 first flight take off at Paine Field, Everett Washington on June 12, 1994. The flight, flown by Chief Pilot John Cashman and Director of Flight Test Captain Ken Higgins, lasted three hours and 48 minutes. The helicopter in the background was a photo platform for the first flight take off. (Boeing/Denise Blangy)

Another view of lift off for first flight on June 12, 1994. Paine Field in Everett Washington was the location for take off and landing of the first flight. Later, test aircraft landed at the Boeing Field flight test center after taking off from the wide-body factory at Everett. (Boeing)

Landing from first flight under cloudy skies at Paine Field, Everett, Washington. Note the thrust reversers in use. All tests went well. Pilots reported exceptional trim and excellent handling qualities. (Boeing/Denise Blangy)

ETOPS

Extended-range Twin-engine OPerationS (ETOPS) is a very important qualification to airline customers. According to Gary Vassallo, Manager of ETOPS programs for the 777 Division of Boeing Commercial Airplane Company, "The importance of early ETOPS to Boeing, the airlines, and the flying public is threefold:

"It provides an advantage for Boeing: the ability to define optimum airplane configurations without arbitrarily requiring three or four engines.

"It provides an immediate strategic advantage for airlines. They can fly the routes that have the greatest commercial value with the most efficient airplanes, without needing to gather multi-year experience for ETOPS approval.

"And it provides an opportunity for airline passengers: the ability to enjoy 777 comfort over long distances at the introduction of service."

ETOPS approval is required for twin-engine aircraft (like the Boeing 777) to fly routes across water that are more than one hour from a suitable alternate landing field at any given time on the flight. The aircraft and airline must be ETOPS approved in the event that the aircraft has to divert to an alternate airport on only one engine or while experiencing an essential-system problem.

Ultimately, this requirment determines the routes airlines can fly with twin-engine aircraft. The goal of Boeing and the three engine manufacturers was to deliver the aircraft ETOPS-qualified at the start of airline revenue service - the so-called out-of-the-box ETOPS. Normally ETOPS approval is issued by the Federal Aviation Administration (FAA) and European Joint Airworthiness Authorities (JAA) after several years of in-service operation to prove the required reliability.

Vassallo describes obtaining ETOPS approval for each engine/airframe combination as a twofold process. "First, regulatory agencies like the FAA and JAA grant ETOPS Type Design approval for a specific twin-engine airplane based on its reliable design and testing, which demonstrates ETOPS capability. In the case of the 777, the agencies also wanted to know that the airplane's support products (training, manuals, spares, etc.) were service-ready.

"Then these agencies must grant approval to specific airlines to operate an ETOPS-approved airplane. Airline ETOPS operational approval is based on the demonstrated capability of the airline's maintenance, flight operations, flight planning, and training. Like the airplane's Type Design approval, the airline's support products must also be service-ready to support operational approval."

On June 7, 1995 the Boeing 777-200 started service on its first revenue flight for United Airlines with full ETOPS approval. The flight took three hours and marked the first time in aviation history that a commercial jetliner went into service with full ETOPS approval.

To obtain ETOPS approval this early was no easy task. It began during the design phase of the aircraft, engines, and systems. Boeing, the engine manufacturers, and the suppliers of systems and components all worked together to design and produce a complete aircraft that was more reliable from the start. The aircraft, when delivered to the airline customer, came with the reliability that would normally evolve from changes made during the initial two years in airline service.

Additional testing, to an extent not previously accomplished on other airliner development programs, was necessary to prove that the 777 was reliable enough for ETOPS approval from the

Fire trucks stand by at the end of the 100 percent Refused Takeoff (RTO) test at Edwards Air Force Base California on Jan 31, 1995. Brake temperatures reach 3000 degrees and get red hot during this test. (Boeing/ Brett Olson).

Before the tires explode from the heat induced pressure build-up at the end of the RTO test, safety fuse plugs on the tires blow. Tires, wheels, and brakes are literally destroyed in this test. (Boeing/Brett Olson)

*AIRLINER*TECH
SERIES

$750,000 worth of wheels and brakes are destroyed in the 100 percent RTO test. The wheel and brake assemblies must be changed before the aircraft can be moved. (Boeing/Brett Olson)

beginning. Testing of aircraft, engines, and systems occurred in test labs, on test benches, in wind tunnels, in engine run test facilities, in climatic chambers, on flying test beds, and during flight test of the complete aircraft system. Three of the ten aircraft in the flight test program were dedicated to ETOPS qualification testing. Aircraft WA004, with Pratt & Whitney engines, flew 1000 cycles for ETOPS validation. One cycle included an engine start, taxi, and takeoff followed by climb, cruise, descent, approach, landing, and engine shutdown. In accordance with requirements, the aircraft was maintained and operated like a "mini-airline". This included the use of in-service airline procedures and manuals.

1,000 cycles simulates more than a year of 777 commercial service. The 1,000 cycles flown by WA004 took the aircraft from hot, dry desert climates to freezing Arctic climates. During the reliability demonstration, the test aircraft was flown on eight divert flights. One engine and some systems were shut down to prove that the complete aircraft was capable of making a three-hour diversion to an alternate field. During the last 90 cycles of the validation flights, 777 WA004 was operated and maintained by United Airlines personnel, with no assistance from the Boeing personnel on board. This part of the validation process proved the airline's ETOPS capability; i.e., that the airline could operate and maintain the aircraft to ETOPS standards. The FAA participated in all 1,000 flights.

Boeing 777-200 WA102, which used Rolls Royce Trent engines, was the ETOPS test aircraft for validating the Rolls Royce configured -200. WA077, which used GE90 engines, was the ETOPS test aircraft for validating the GE90 configured -200.

FLIGHT TESTING

A total of ten 777-200 aircraft were used in the flight test program. Three different engines were available as airline customer options and testing and certification were required for each

Tail dragging during VMU tests at Edwards Air Force Base on September 15, 1994. The Velocity Minimum Unstick tests are conducted to determine the aircraft's minimum takeoff speed. This test requires the aircraft's tail to come in contact with the runway prior to takeoff. (Boeing/Bob Carnahan)

Close up view of the tail skid during the VMU test at Edwards Air Force Base. The tail is protected during the VMU tests by a tailskid with a replaceable oak block wear pad. (Boeing)

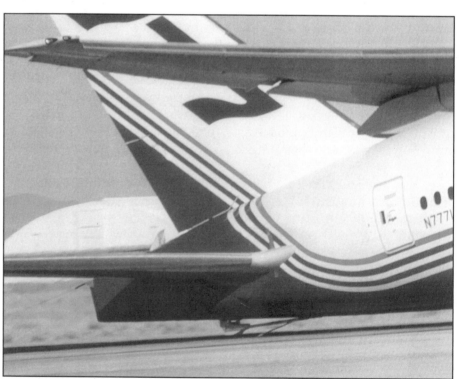

engine-airframe combination. Since the launch customer, United Airlines, selected Pratt & Whitney PW4084 engines, the first five aircraft used P&W engines during initial testing.

P&W engine testing was done on aircraft numbers WA001, WA002, WA003, WA004 and WA005. 1,490 tests were run on these five aircraft, including basic aircraft testing. GE90 engine testing was done on aircraft numbers WA076, WA077 and WA 078: 366 tests were run on these three aircraft. Rolls Royce engine testing was done on aircraft numbers WA101 and

AIRLINER TECH
SERIES

Wet runway tests, simulating adverse weather runway conditions, are used to check aero performance and braking. Edwards Air Force Base water tankers have applied 27,000 gallons of water on the desert runway. (Boeing)

WA102: 299 tests were run on these two aircraft. In all, a total of 2,155 tests were accomplished on the ten aircraft.

The 777 Program Schedule shown on page 49 is a good overview of the -200 development and certification flight test spans for nine of the ten test aircraft. Not shown is WA078, which did twenty-seven tests with GE90 engines. Flight testing for the FAA Type Certificate for the P&W-powered 777 was accomplished in only ten-and-a-half months, using four of the P&W powered aircraft.

FIRST FLIGHT

Flight test aircraft WA001 rolled out on April 9, 1994. After completing ground and preflight tests, the aircraft made its first flight on June 12, 1994. John Cashman, 777 Chief Pilot and Captain Ken Higgins, Director of Flight Test for Boeing Commercial Airplane Group, flew first flight from Paine Field at Everett, Washington. The flight, which lasted three hours and forty-eight minutes, included a handling qualities check, landing gear cycling in both the normal and alternate modes, and check-out of hydraulic, electrical and pneumatic systems. Other tests accomplished included approaches to stall, operation of the flight control system in both the Normal and Direct modes, an engine shutdown and windmill relight, and an abbreviated version of the initial checkout flight done on all Boeing aircraft on their first factory flights. All tests went well. The pilots reported exceptional trim and excellent handling qualities in both flight control modes.

Flight test crews typically consist of the pilots, a test director, a weights/operations engineer, two instrumentation engineers, and flight test analysis and program staff engineers from the disciplines associated with the tests being conducted. Supplier technical representatives may also be on board, as engine manufacturer reps may be part of the test crew during engine tests. The type of testing planned and its associated hazard level dictate the number of participants and test composition. Basic airworthiness and flutter testing is done with a minimum crew of two pilots. Telemetry (TM) is used during these minimum crew flights to transmit real time data to the ground station, where all the critical parameters are monitored and recorded. After this initial airworthiness clearance, crew sizes generally range from eight to twenty-five.

Water spray ingestion testing is accomplished at Glasgow, Montana on July 30, 1994, on WA002. The nose gear is run through a trough of water to evaluate effects of the water spray ingestion. (Boeing/Joe Parke)

T-38 chase aircraft with WA076, the first British Airways 777, during flutter tests with GE engines, February 17, 1995. Each engine-airframe combination for the three different engine options requires a complete set of tests. (Boeing/ Debra O'Brezar)

T-33 chase aircraft with WA076 during flutter tests. Chase aircraft are used for first flights and critical high speed tests where an external observer is necessary. (Boeing/Joe Parke)

FLIGHT TEST TASKS BY AIRCRAFT
WA001

The primary tests on the number one aircraft were flutter tests, which test the structural dynamic response of the aircraft, aerodynamic performance development, and certification. Following standard procedure, tests were performed during takeoff, cruise, maneuvering, stalls, and landing. Stability and control development and certification testing validated the aircraft's flying qualities over a range of weights and center of gravity envelopes. Preliminary propulsion evaluation looked at the handling and starting characteristics of the engine, fuel consumption, and operation of the engine control systems and engine accessory components. Aircraft performance was measured by the on-board instrumentation system.

Evaluation of aircraft systems and autopilot development testing were also done on WA001. The test aircraft totaled 751 flight hours and 730 ground test hours.

WA002

Flight test aircraft WA002 rolled out on June 12, 1994 and made its first flight on July 15, 1994. Primary flight test tasks were propulsion development, aerodynamic and stability and control development, avionics development and certification, systems development and certification, community noise certification, and natural icing certification. WA002 totaled 656 flight hours and 770 ground test hours.

WA003

Flight test aircraft WA003 rolled out on June 29, 1994 and made its first flight on August 2, 1994. Primary flight test tasks were propulsion development and certification, aerodynamic development, avionics development and certification, systems development and certification, autopilot development and certification, and flight loads survey. The test aircraft's 830 ground test hours were almost double its 432 total flight hours.

WA004

Flight test aircraft WA004 rolled out on August 24, 1994 and made first flight on October 28, 1994. This test aircraft was dedicated to ETOPS and service ready testing. It flew a total of 1283 hours and underwent 724 hours of ground tests. A total of 1107 cycles were flown during the ETOPS testing.

WA005

Flight test aircraft WA005 rolled out on September 22, 1994 and made its first flight on November 11, 1994. Primary flight test tasks were avionics certification, systems certification,

EMI/Lightning/HIRF (HIgh-energy Radiated Field) testing, cabin-noise testing, and fire and smoke detection. This test aircraft had the lowest number of flight hours (278), and the highest number of ground test hours (913), because of the types of tests that were run.

Pratt & Whitney PW4084 engines powered all five aircraft. Test tasks involved development and certification testing, in that order. According to Cliff Moore, Director of Flight Test Engineering: "Approximately one-third of the flight tests were for development and validation, with two-thirds of the testing for certification requirements, when you include ETOPS certification. Without the ETOPS flight hours counted, the ratio is just the reverse, with two-thirds development and one-third certification flying."

As the above statement illustrates, ETOPS qualification played a large role in 777 testing. FAA and JAA Type Certificates were issued for the P&W powered Boeing 777-200 on April 19, 1995.

GE90 FLIGHT TESTS

Flight testing with General Electric GE90 engines was accomplished on aircraft numbers WA076, WA077, and WA078. These aircraft flew a combined total of 2,025 flight hours.

WA076

Flight test aircraft WA076 rolled out on November 14, 1994 and made its first flight on February 2, 1995. Primary flight test tasks were flutter, aerodynamic performance evaluation, propulsion and systems validation and certification, community noise certification, HIRF, and JAA (European Joint Aviation Authorities) evaluation and certification. WA076 totaled 482 flight hours and 399 ground test hours.

WA077

Flight test aircraft WA077 rolled out on January 13, 1995. ETOPS testing on this aircraft started on March 30, 1996 and it made its first flight on April 11, 1995. Primary flight test task for this air-

craft was support of GE engine development and ETOPS and service ready testing. WA077 totaled 1,457 flight hours and 546 ground test hours. ETOPS testing, which included 1,000 cycles, took up 1,050 hours of total flight time.

WA078

Flight test aircraft WA078's first flight was on September 1, 1995. WA078 totaled 86 flight hours and 16 ground test hours for GE engine testing.

A number of tests done on the first five Pratt & Whitney powered aircraft were repeated on the GE90 and Rolls Royce powered aircraft. Aero performance, primary and secondary flight controls, stability and control, flight deck, avionics, auto flight controls, hydraulic/landing gear systems, and structures tests were all repeated, as were flight management computer system, aircraft noise, propulsion and fuel systems, maintenance manual validation, environmental control system, electrical, payloads and ETOPS.

Additional testing verified and certified the compatibility of both GE's and Rolls Royce's engine designs with the Boeing 777 aircraft and its systems. Testing on the three GE powered test aircraft led to FAA and JAA Type Certification and ETOPS approval on November 9, 1995.

RR TRENT ENGINE FLIGHT TESTS

Flight testing with the Rolls Royce Trent 800 engines for the 777-200 was accomplished on flight test aircraft numbers WA101 and WA102. These aircraft flew a combined total of 1,961 hours.

WA101

Flight test aircraft WA101 rolled out on January 13, 1995 and made its first flight on April 11, 1995. Primary tests on this aircraft were flutter, aerodynamic performance evaluation, propulsion and systems validation and certification, community noise certification, High Energy Radiated Field (HIRF) testing, and JAA Evaluation

and certification. WA101 totaled 633 flight hours and 457 ground test hours.

WA102

Flight test aircraft WA102 rolled out on June 29, 1995 and made its first flight on November 9, 1995. WA102 was the ETOPS and service ready test aircraft. WA102 totaled 1,328 flight hours and 415 ground test hours. ETOPS testing took up 1,116 of the total 1,328 flight hours, with a total of 1,016 cycles flown.

Testing on the two Rolls Royce powered test aircraft led to FAA and JAA type certification and ETOPS approval on February 28, 1996.

RTO TESTS

Flight tests conducted on the basic 777-200 "A-Market" version included tests at parameters to meet "B-Market" certification, the Increased Gross Weight (IGW) version of the 777, which reduced the amount of testing required on the -200 IGW. Maximum energy Refused Takeoff (RTO) testing, for example, was accomplished at the B-Market maximum gross weight of 632,500 pounds, instead of the A-Market weight of 535,000 pounds. Engine thrust rating for this test, which ensures that the aircraft's braking systems will be able to stop the heaviest 777 before the end of the runway, if take-off was refused just before lift-off, was increased from the normal 77,000 pounds to 88,000 pounds. RTO tests were accomplished at Edwards Air Force Base in California - just in case the base's 15,000-foot runway was needed! The RTO test was done with worn brakes to simulate real-world use. There was a tremendous amount of heat generated: during 100 percent RTO, the brakes glowed red-hot.

Part of the test involved brake ability to absorb heat without setting the aircraft on fire. After the aircraft had completed braking, no external action could be taken for five minutes. This simulated the response time of the fire department in a real situation. After

U.S. Air Force KC-135 tanker during icing tests on WA077, October 6, 1995. This specially modified KC-135 based at Edwards Air Force Base, California, carries large water tanks in the fuselage and uses a special controllable spray nozzle in place of the normal refueling probe. (Boeing/Jeff Rumsey)

RTO, the aircraft taxied off the runway. Brake temperatures went to about 3000Co at that point. Heat caused tire pressures to build up until tires were ready to explode. But the fuse plugs did their job and blew first, causing tires to deflate before they could explode. After the fuse plugs blew, the fire department cooled the brakes down with water. $750,000 worth of wheels and brakes were purposely destroyed in this test - part of the flight testing that assures a safe product for the customer.

VMU TESTS

Velocity Minimum Unstick (VMU) tests are designed to determine the absolute minimum speed at which an aircraft, with all engines operating, will take off and maintain a positive rate of climb. This speed is used to determine V2 safe take-off speed.

Preventative measures are taken to protect the bottom of the fuselage and to determine when the tail actually touches the runway during these tests. A long rod, which signals the cockpit, touches the ground first. A laser-measuring device transmits the tail-to-runway distance to the cockpit to aid the pilot in determining tail position during the VMU tests. The tail skid is comprised of a lever attached to an oak block. After the lever is compressed, the wood block becomes the tail skid rubbing surface between the bottom of the fuselage and the runway. The oak block is changed frequently during these tests, since it quickly wears down.

A flight test tail skid was used on the underside of the fuselage on the -200 for protection during minimum takeoff speed rotation tests. In these tests, the pilot holds the yoke aft during the takeoff roll to determine the minimum unstick speed of the aircraft. Tail dragging usually occurs.

WET RUNWAY TESTING

Two types of tests involve wet runway testing. As Andy Hammer, Lead Flight Test Engineer, Boeing Commercial Airplane Group, describes them: "The basic wet runway test is for aero performance and braking tests. Here, stopping distances are determined on a wet runway, typically accomplished at an airfield like Edwards Air Force Base, California; Moses Lake, Washington; or Glasgow, Montana. At these locations, trucks can apply water on the runway for the tests without interfering with commercial operations."

Andy Hammer explains the second type of wet runway test, "Water ingestion testing is set up by building a three-quarter-inch deep trough on the runway, typically using foam, and filling it with water. The nose gear of the aircraft is run through the trough at increasing aircraft speeds, in increments of 10 knots, to determine the critical engine water ingestion speed. Critical ingestion speed is based on the amount of water thrown toward the inlet and is documented by instrumentation video cameras mounted externally on the aircraft. Airfields for wet runway tests are also used for the water ingestion tests."

CHASE AIRCRAFT

Boeing Commercial Airplane Group Flight Test has three aircraft for chase duties on their various flight test programs. A Northrop T-38 Talon and two Lockheed T-33 Shooting Stars are currently used. Chase aircraft are typically flown on first flights and critical high speed and flutter tests, where an external observer can be essential. An external observer can also be useful dur-

During icing tests behind the KC-135 tanker, water spray forms an ice cloud. The ice cloud is the result of the correct combination of cold temperature at altitude, and the controllable water droplet size from the tanker. (Boeing/Jeff Rumsey).

ing icing tests, accomplished with a KC-135 tanker that sprays water at an altitude/temperature combination to create a controllable ice cloud. Crew for a chase flight typically consists of an engineering test pilot and a photographer.

RECORDS and AWARDS

The 777 received The National Aeronautic Association's award for the top aeronautical achievement of 1995, the Collier Trophy, for "designing, manufacturing and placing into service the worlds most technologically advanced airline transport".

The National Air and Space Smithsonian Institution's 1996 Trophy for Current Achievement was awarded to the 777 development team for: "reshaping the way the industry builds airplanes by developing 'working together' relationships with the airlines, partners, suppliers, and all who designed and built the 777 to create the most advanced and service-ready twin-jet in commercial aviation history."

In nominating the Boeing 777 team for the Current Achievement award, the Society of Flight Test Engineers stated that the 777 program: "Has been a model of efficiency, utilizing the very latest technology, as well as developing a wide range of new technologies to design, fabricate, flight test and, finally, to certify the aircraft for international use."

In April 1997, the 777-200 IGW broke both speed and distance world records, flying the fastest and farthest of its size and class on a flight from Seattle to Kuala Lumpur, Malaysia. The record it established for the Great Circle Distance Without Landing was 12,455.34 statute miles. Another record, Speed Around the World, Eastbound, was set on the return flight by traveling the Seattle-Kuala Lumpur-Seattle route at an average speed of 553 mph. The Airbus A340-211 previously held both records. The Federations Aeronautique Internationale (FAI), the world aviation-record governing board, and the FAI's U.S. counterpart, the National Aeronautic Association (NAA), certified the new records.

AIRLINE OPERATIONS

United Airlines was the initial launch customer for the Boeing 777-200 with an order for thirty-four 777s and an option for thirty-four more. On May 17, 1995, United took delivery of its first 777 in a special ceremony at Boeing Field in Seattle. Revenue service began on June 7, between London's Heathrow Airport and Dulles Airport, Washington D.C.

In 1934, United Airlines took delivery of a twin-engine, all-metal, 10-passenger aircraft, the Boeing 247.

Powered by two 550-horsepower Pratt & Whitney Wasp engines, the 247 was as advanced, in its day, as the 777 is today. An aerodynamically clean all-metal aircraft that was fifty percent faster than its competitors, the 247 required two engines instead of three. Like many tri-motors of the 1930s, it had the latest revolutions in aeronautical technology, including retractable landing gear and an autopilot.

It is interesting to compare the spacious three-class, twin-aisle cabin of

the United 777 with the 247, which seated ten passengers. When walking up the 247's single aisle, one had to step over the main wing spar, which ran across the cabin. The 777's 292 passenger configuration consists of twelve First Class seats arranged in 2-2-2 pairs with a total width of fifty-seven inches - a full three inches wider than current First Class seating on the 747 and 767. Connoisseur Class features forty-nine seats in a 2-3-2 configuration with adjustable head rests and extendible leg

A 1934 United Airlines Boeing 247D parked next to United's current airliner, the Boeing 777-200, offers an interesting contrast. Two Pratt & Whitney engines power each aircraft. The aircraft were delivered to United 60 years apart. (Boeing/Ken Dejarlais)

The spacious first class section of the 777 has two aisles with six-across seating and individual entertainment systems at each seat. The high ceilings and open airy cabin provide a stark contrast to the 1934 step-across-the-wing-spar interior of the 247. (Boeing)

rests. Economy Class seats 231, configured in a 2-5-2 design.

United's in-flight entertainment system, found at each seat, offers six channels of video, nineteen channels of CD quality audio, video games, and telecommunications services. Video games range from card, board, and arcade offerings to sports, puzzles, and children's games. Two channels of video are reserved for feature films, including a dual-language channel for flights going to and from non-English speaking countries. In the Economy Class section, video screens are on the seat backs. In First Class and Connoisseur Class seats, the video display pulls up out of the armrest.

Japan Airlines

Japan Airlines (JAL) took delivery of its first 777-200 on February 15, 1996 with entry into service on April 26, 1996, between Tokyo's Haneda *(text continued on page 69)*

Delivery ceremony of United's first 777 with a flyby of the number one test aircraft, WA001. Notice the Boeing 247 on the ramp to the right of United's 777. The ceremony was in front of the Museum of Flight in Seattle. (Boeing)

777 IN DRAMATIC COLOR

Color photography gives the opportunity to present an aircraft in it's diverse environments with brilliant realism. Here, the Boeing 777 is shown in assorted activities including test flights with chase aircraft, laying contrails at high altitude, and braking to a stop at the end of an RTO with smoking, red-hot brakes. The color displays in the modern flight deck are featured along with some dramatic lighting techniques used on the engine in the test cell.

First flight of the Boeing 777-200 on June 12, 1994, flown by Capt. John Cashman, 777 chief pilot, and Capt. Ken Higgins, director of Flight Test for Boeing. The Northrop T-38 chase aircraft belongs to Boeing Commercial Airplane Group Flight Test and is used on first flights and critical high speed and flutter tests where an external observer is essential. (Boeing)

100 percent refused takeoff tests at maximum gross weight result in brake temperatures reaching 3000 degrees and glowing red-hot. Wheels and brakes are destroyed in this test and must be replaced on the runway or taxi-way before the aircraft can taxi back in. This test demonstrates to the FAA that the aircraft's brakes, in their most diminished state, can still stop a fully loaded 777 if there is a need to abort a takeoff. (Boeing)

Fire department cools down the 3000 degree red-hot brakes at the end of the 100 percent RTO test at Edwards Air Force Base in California. 14,000 gallons of water are applied to the brakes and deflated tires after waiting five minutes to simulate normal response time. (Boeing)

GE's 747 flying testbed with the GE90 engine on the left inboard position, ready for take off at Mojave, California. Notice the small amount of ground clearance, which is only 13 inches, on the test engine for the 777. (GE Aircraft Engines)

Engine icing tests on 777 WA077. Photo from the KC-135 tanker's boom operator position shows the spray array boom. Water is sprayed that becomes a controlled ice cloud due to the cold air temperature at the predetermined altitude. (Boeing/Jeff Rumsey)

PW4084 on the engine test-stand at Pratt & Whitney's West Palm Beach Florida facility. Colored lighting at sunset produces a dramatic color photo. (Pratt & Whitney)

AIRLINER TECH
SERIES

Water ingestion tests at Glasgow, Montana, are used to determine how much water spray, from a wet runway, goes into the engine inlet. (Boeing/Joe Parke)

British Airways 777-200 powered by General Electric GE90 engines. (British Airways)

Flight deck of the 777-200 is best presented in color. There are six flat panel, liquid crystal color displays for the two pilot crew. The fly-by-wire flight control system retains the familiar yoke, and feel forces in the control system are maintained to give the pilot the same type cues he would get from a mechanical flight control system. (Boeing)

Roll out of the 777-300, the longest commercial jetliner in the world, on September 8, 1997. Cathay Pacific Airways of Hong Kong will be the first customer to take delivery of the -300. For a size comparison, the hangar doors with the colorful sunset picture are the size of an American football field. (Boeing)

The first 777-300, WB501, lands at Boeing Field, Seattle at the end of the four hour first flight, followed by the T-33 chase aircraft. The successful flight was flown October 16, 1997 by Chief 777 Pilot Frank Santoni and Chief Pilot for Boeing Commercial Airplane Group John Cashman. (Boeing/Herb Gandy)

777-200, WA076 on a flutter flight with a T-33 chase aircraft on February 17, 1995. (Boeing/Joe Parke)

777-200 WA001 leaves a contrail during high altitude flutter testing on December 12, 1994. Contrails, or condensation trails, are the visible trail of condensed water vapor or ice particles left behind an aircraft. The engine exhaust-moisture is formed by the ejection of water vapor from the engine into a cold atmosphere. (Boeing/Joe Parke)

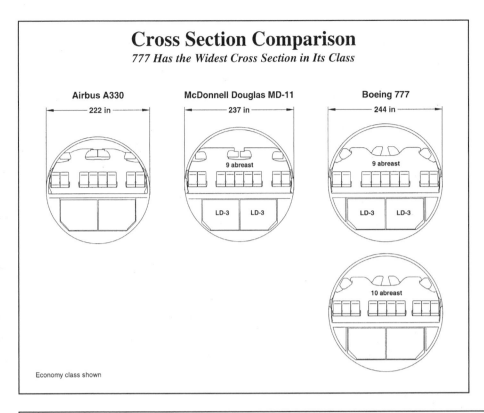

Cross Section Comparison
777 Has the Widest Cross Section in Its Class

Airbus A330 — 222 in

McDonnell Douglas MD-11 — 237 in — 9 abreast — LD-3 LD-3

Boeing 777 — 244 in — 9 abreast — LD-3 LD-3

10 abreast

Economy class shown

Comparison of the 777 cross section with the competition. The 777 has a wider cross section than either the Airbus A330 or the McDonnell Douglas MD-11. (Boeing)

(text continued from page 64)
Airport and Kagoshima on the southernmost island of Kyushu. As of August 26, 1997 JAL had five -200 aircraft in service. Firm orders for ten additional 777's include five -200s (plus options for ten more) and five -300s (delivery to begin in 1998). JAL calls its 777 fleet "Star Jets", and each aircraft is named after a major constellation. The first is named "Sirius". Sirius, located near the constellation of Orion, is the brightest star in the sky.

JAL's 389 passenger seating configuration includes 12 super seats in domestic First Class and 377 nine-

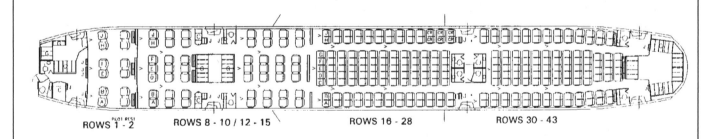

B777-200 XI
12F/49C/231Y = 292

ZONE A - FIRST
12 SEATS

ZONE A/B - CONNOISSEUR
21 SEATS/28SEATS

ZONE B - ECONOMY
117 SEATS

ZONE C - ECONOMY
114 SEATS

ROWS 1 - 2   PILOT REST   ROWS 8 - 10 / 12 - 15   ROWS 16 - 28   ROWS 30 - 43

LEGEND

G	GALLEY	W	WINDOW EXIT
J	FLIGHT ATTENDANT JUMPSEAT	X	PERMANENT TIEDOWN
L	LAVATORY	Φ	RETRACTABLE TIEDOWN
C	CLOSET	CR	CREW REST
V	VIDEO MONITOR/LCD/SCREEN	DF	DUTY FREE
M	MISCELLANEOUS STOWAGE	CL	CART LIFT

United's cabin arrangement. This grouping has 12 First Class seats, 49 Connoisseur Class seats and 231 Economy class seats. (United Airlines)

United Airlines 777-200 landing at Chicago O'Hare, September 1996. Bulge on the bottom of the fuselage, where the landing gear wheel well is located, can be seen in this view. Notice that the landing gear doors are closed after the gear has been extended. (Tom Pesch)

N767UA taking off from Chicago O'Hare airport, July, 1996. Notice the 13 degree tilt of the six wheel main landing gear. (Tom Pesch)

772UA in flight. United's initial order was for 34 aircraft, with options for an additional 34. (United Airlines)

N776UA at Denver International airport. Photo was taken in June 1996, a year after United took delivery of their first 777-200. (Stephen Griffin)

abreast Economy Class seats in a 3-3-3 configuration, with two aisles. As of August 1997, JAL is only using their -200's on domestic routes, which include Tokyo-Sapporo, Tokyo-Osaka, Tokyo-Nagasaki, Tokyo-Kumaoto and Tokyo-Kagoshima. JAL uses the -200 and -300 primarily on medium-density regional and trunk domestic routes.

JAL selected Pratt & Whitney PW4090 engines for its five Boeing 777-300 aircraft. The twelve-engine order (two for each aircraft and two spares) is worth approximately $140 million. The engine and aircraft orders combined total approximately $800 million, averaging $11.66 million per engine and $132 million per aircraft.

British Airways

In November 1995, British Airways (BA) took delivery of its first -200, with GE90 engines. At the Paris Airshow on June 20, 1997, BA announced an order for five additional Boeing 777s, bringing its total order to twenty-three.

BA uses a three-class passenger configuration on its Boeing 777s. First Cabin has its own unique fully flat flying beds: seventeen on aircraft going to the Middle East and fourteen on North America-UK flights. Club World cabin has a seven-across seating arrangement in a 2-3-2 configuration that uses the airline's "cradle seat", and World Traveler cabin has a nine-across seating

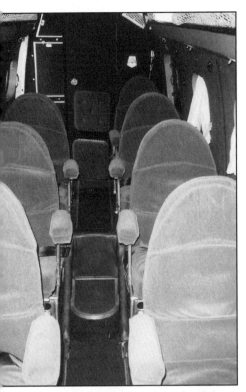

Ten passenger Boeing 247D had the main wing spar running across the cabin. The step in the aisle made it easier for the passengers to get across the spar. (Author)

arrangement in 3-3-3 configuration.

BA in-flight entertainment features individual television screens for each seat in every cabin. Passengers in First Class have personal video players, while those in Club World can choose between eight channels. In the arm of every seat is a fax port and telephone.

Cathay Pacific

Cathay Pacific took delivery of their first -200 on May 10, 1996 with entry into service on May 17,1996. As of September 1997, Cathay Pacific had placed firm orders for eleven 777s, with options for ten additional -200s. The Cathay Pacific -200 was the first 777 powered by the Rolls Royce Trent 877 engine. It is currently being used on regional routes between Hong Kong and Bangkok, Seoul, and Taipei, and on medium-haul routes to Bahrain and Dubai.

Cathay Pacific is the initial launch customer for the -300. Roll out

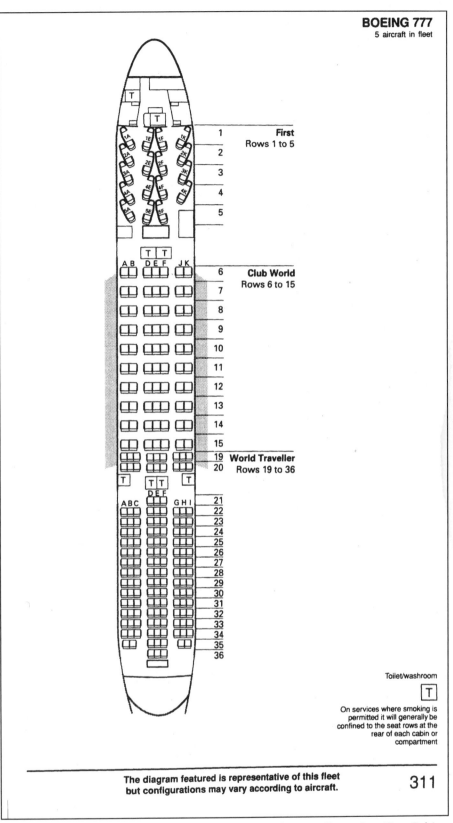

BOEING 777
5 aircraft in fleet

1	**First** Rows 1 to 5
6	**Club World** Rows 6 to 15
19	**World Traveller** Rows 19 to 36

Toilet/washroom

T

On services where smoking is permitted it will generally be confined to the seat rows at the rear of each cabin or compartment

The diagram featured is representative of this fleet but configurations may vary according to aircraft.

311

Cabin configuration for British Airways -200 three class configuration. First Cabin has unique flying beds that go fully flat. (British Airways)

British Airways 777-200 in flight. BA has ordered a total of twenty-three 777s. (British Airways)

British Airways 777s are powered by GE90 engines. BA was the initial launch customer for the GE90. (British Airways)

occurred on September 8, 1997 at Paine Field in Everett, Washington. Cathay ordered a total of seven -300s, to be delivered between May 1998 and October 1999. Planned for use on routes to Japan, Taipei, Bangkok and Seoul, Cathay's -300's are powered by the Rolls Royce Trent 892 engines.

Cathay Pacific's -200 passenger configuration of 336 seats includes forty-three Business Class and 293 Economy Class seats. The seating for its 367-passenger -300s will be in two

Japan Airline's 777-200 in-flight. In addition to the five 777s currently in service, JAL has orders for 10 more. This includes five -300s, plus options for ten more 777's. (Japan Airlines)

Flight simulator for the 777 operated by Japan Airlines. Check pilot's seat and control panels are located to the left in this photo. Various flight scenarios can be set up from the instructor/check pilot's panel to provide realistic unannounced emergencies for flight training and currency checks in the simulator. (Japan Airlines)

Exterior view of Japan Airlines Flight Simulator. The 777 cockpit in the previous photo is inside this enclosure. (Japan Airlines)

Economy class seats have individual video screens in the seat backs. In addition to six video and nineteen audio channels, video games range from card, board, and arcade games to children's games. (United Airlines)

British Airways 777. Notice the wing tip deflection in-flight. (British Airways)

Cathay Pacific 777-200 at Everett, Washington. Cathay Pacific has ordered eleven 777s, including seven -300s, with options for ten more 777s. (Boeing)

classes: 80 in Business Class and 287 in Economy. Cathay Pacific's -200s have eight-channel personal TVs in each Business Class seat. The -300s will be delivered with nine-channel personal TVs in every Business Class seat, and six-channel personal TVs in every Economy Class seat.

All Nippon Airways

All Nippon Airways (ANA), another launch customer, was the first airline in the Asian-Pacific region to take delivery of the Boeing -200. Special ceremonies were held on October 4, 1995 at Seattle's Museum of Flight. "We're delivering the 777 ready for service," said Boeing President Phil Condit, who hosted the delivery ceremony. "With the contributions of ANA and the other 'working together' partners, we are convinced that we have created the right airplane, for the right market, at the right time. The 777 has proven this by capturing over 75 percent of its market."

Echoing these comments, ANA's President and Chief Executive Officer Seiji Fukatsu said, "ANA has influenced

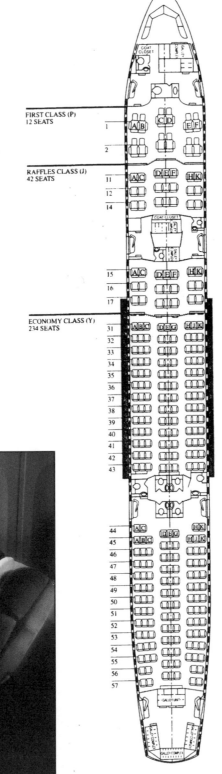

First Class seating on United has 64 inches of clearance between passenger rows, allowing full reclining. Video screen pulls up out of the arm rest. (United Airlines)

Cabin configuration for Singapore Airlines three class 777-200. There are 12 seats in First class, 42 seats in Raffles class, and 234 seats in economy class. (Singapore Airlines)

the design of the aircraft in ways big and small, from the locations of the fueling system to the washroom fittings. Our 'working together' partnership has made us just as proud as Boeing of the final product. As the first Asian carrier to take delivery of the 777, we are confident that it will be the aircraft that will take us into the 21st Century."

ANA's plans called for the 777 to be the backbone of its domestic routes, which commenced in December 1995. ANA's domestic system, which carries over 34 million passengers annually, consists primarily of one to two hour flights connecting high-density points. ANA began revenue service on

PW4084 powered 777 is delivered to All Nippon Airways. ANA has ordered a total of twenty-eight 777s, including ten -300s. ANA was the first airline to take delivery of the -200 in the Asia-Pacific region. (Pratt & Whitney)

The first Rolls-Royce Trent 800 powered Boeing 777 for Cathay Pacific lands at Boeing Field, Seattle. Cathay Pacific was the launch customer for the Rolls Royce powered 777. (Rolls-Royce)

December 23, 1995 with Flight No. NH 15 between Tokyo (Haneda) and Osaka (Itami). ANA has ordered a total of 28 Boeing 777s powered by Pratt & Whitney PW4074 engines. Eighteen are -200s and ten are -300s.

Singapore Airlines

Singapore Airlines (SIA) took delivery of its first 777-200 on May 6, 1997 with entry into service on May 15, 1997, on Flight SQ154 from Singapore to Jakarta. To help celebrate its 50th Anniversary Jubilee in 1997, SIA named its -200s "Jubilee 777s". As of September 1997, Singapore Airlines had placed firm orders for thirty-four 777s, with options for another forty-three. The SIA -200s are powered by the Rolls Royce Trent 877 engines. Six of the firm orders and ten of the options are for Singapore Aircraft Leasing Enterprise (SALE). The engine selection for these planes has yet to be determined.

SIA's Boeing -200 configuration for 288 passengers includes twelve in First Class, forty-two in Raffles Class, and 234 in Economy Class. In First Class, all seats feature a six-way adjustable head-rest and a four-way electrical lumbar support system. Seats are six across in a 2-2-2 arrangement with two aisles. Raffles Class features a four way adjustable headrest with "wings", two-way adjustable lumbar support, and electrical powered leg-

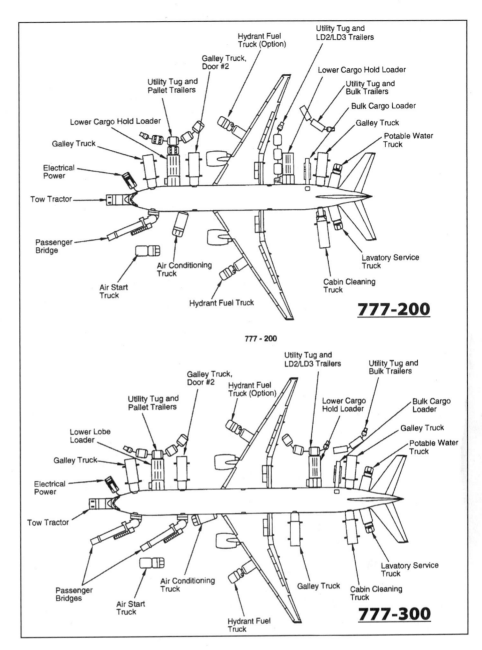

777-200

777-300

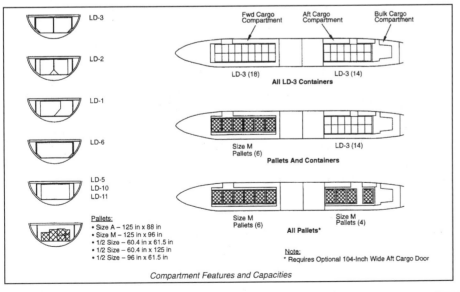

Compartment Features and Capacities

Ground support and servicing equipment locations at the aircraft for the 777-200 and 777-300. All of the various ground operations that go on for a turn around flight have servicing locations that do not interfere with each other. (Boeing)

Cargo compartment locations and capacities for the 777-200. The three cargo compartments in the lower deck are the forward, aft, and bulk compartments. (Boeing)

rest. Seats are seven across in a 2-3-2 configuration. Economy class seats have adjustable head-rests with foldable "ears" and foot rests, and are nine across in a 3-3-3 configuration.

Loading the forward lower cargo hold. Operation of the forward cargo compartment is the same as for the aft, including a single operator. (Boeing/Brett Olson)

Loading the aft lower cargo hold on WA004 during fit checks at Seatac airport. A single operator can control the operation of loading containers and pallets. The operator uses an external joystick and control panel to set the configuration and operate the system. (Boeing/Brett Olson)

Galley truck and lavatory service truck during a fit check on WA004 at Seatac airport, Washington December 18, 1994. Notice how the various functions can occur simultaneously. (Boeing/Brett Olson)

Lower cargo hold loader (on the right) and the bulk cargo loader during fit check on WA004/N773UA at Seatac airport. The bulk cargo compartment holds loose baggage, while the other cargo compartments use pre-loaded containers and pallets. (Boeing/Brett Olson)

China Southern 777-200 landing at Los Angeles International airport. China Southern has ordered six of the GE90 powered -200s. (Stephen Griffin)

China Southern 777 taxiing in at Los Angeles International airport. This is the first of six ordered. (Stephen Griffin)

N768UA landing at Chicago O'Hare airport June, 1997. Distinctive flat shape of the tail cone can be seen in this view, a useful feature for distinguishing the 777 from other twin-engine wide-bodies. (Tom Pesch)

The SIA Jubilee Boeing -200 uses the KrisWorld interactive inflight entertainment and communications system. KrisWorld offers twenty-two channels of video entertainment, twelve audio channels, ten Nintendo games, real-time text news, and destination information on sixteen of the cities in SIA's route network. All classes in the aircraft have this system. In First and Raffles Class, the system's 6.5 inch LCD screens are fitted to each seat's armrest. In Economy, the screens are installed in the seat-backs. Passengers in First Class have access to Active Noise Reducing headphones that eliminate virtually all background noise. In all classes, a personal in-seat KrisFone allows passen-

Rolls Royce Trent 800 powered Emirates and Thai International 777-200s. Emirates has ordered nine -200s. Thai Airways has ordered eight -200s and six -300s. (Rolls-Royce)

gers to telephone anywhere in the world from the air, or simply contact another passenger on the same flight using the seat-to-seat facility.

THE 777-300 - LONGEST AIRLINER IN THE WORLD

The 777-300, the longest commercial jetliner in the world, rolled out of Boeing's Everett, Washington plant on September 8, 1997, marking the completion of manufacturing and the beginning of flight test. Several hundred airline customers and suppliers joined thousands of Boeing employees outside the factory for the celebration.

"The 777-300 is a lot longer, but we planned from the beginning to accommodate all three models of the 777 airplane on the same assembly line," said Ron Ostrowski, Vice President and General Manager of the 777 Program. "Boeing workers began assembling the -300 in early April and five months later rolled out the world's longest commercial jetliner. Their skill and dedication reflect the company's commitment to building the best airplanes in the world."

The -300 is the newest and largest member of the Boeing 777 aircraft family. It is 242 feet 4 inches from nose to tail, which makes it thirty-three feet longer than the -200. The -300 carries twenty percent more passengers than the -200: between 368 and 550 passengers, depending on configuration. The -300 is 10 feet 6 inches longer than the 747-400, although the 747-400 remains the largest commercial jetliner in the world. The 747-400 can carry between 420 and 568 passengers, with a maximum take-off weight of 875,000 pounds and a range of 8,290 statute miles (7,204 nautical miles).

First 777-300 in the final assembly position, where engines and the APU are installed and functional checks are run on the aircraft systems. Notice the additional door position over the wing. (Boeing)

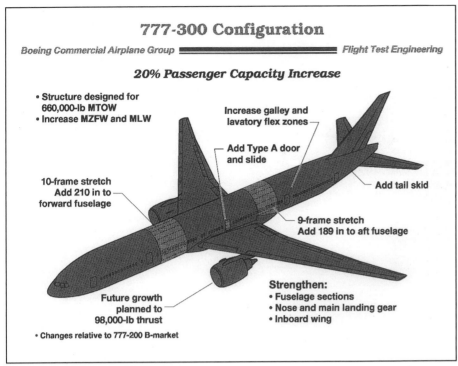

777-300 Configuration

Boeing Commercial Airplane Group ━━━━━ Flight Test Engineering

20% Passenger Capacity Increase

- Structure designed for 660,000-lb MTOW
- Increase MZFW and MLW

Increase galley and lavatory flex zones

Add Type A door and slide

Add tail skid

10-frame stretch
Add 210 in to forward fuselage

9-frame stretch
Add 189 in to aft fuselage

Future growth planned to 98,000-lb thrust

Strengthen:
- Fuselage sections
- Nose and main landing gear
- Inboard wing

- Changes relative to 777-200 B-market

Some significant configuration changes for the -300. Shaded locations show where additional sections were added to the fuselage. Structure design was for a 660,000 pound Maximum Take Off Weight with a corresponding increase in Maximum Zero Fuel Weight and Maximum Landing Weight (MLW). (Boeing)

Pacific Airways. "This aircraft will help Cathay Pacific grow by giving us the ability to add greater capacity to high-frequency regional routes."

Other customers for the -300 include All Nippon Airways, Japan Airlines, Korean Air, Malaysia Airlines, Singapore Airlines, and Thai Airways International. "The airlines of Asia are relying on the 777 family to deliver unsurpassed performance and capability while transforming air travel to, from, and within Asia," said Larry Dickenson, Vice President - Asia Pacific, Boeing Commercial Airplane Group. "We commend Cathay Pacific's leadership and appreciate their confidence in being the launch customer for the 777-300." Typical routes for the -300 include Tokyo-Singapore, Honolulu-Seoul or San Francisco-Tokyo. Engines for the aircraft are certified to 90,000 pounds of thrust and are available from Pratt & Whitney, Rolls Royce, and General Electric.

Maximum take off weight on the -300 is 660,000 pounds. The -300 has the same fuel capacity (45,220 gallons) as the longer-range IGW aircraft, and will serve routes up to 6,550 statute miles (5,700 nautical miles). It satisfies airline demand for an aircraft that can replace early versions of the 747. The -300 has nearly the same passenger capacity and range capability as the 747-100/200 models, burning one-third less fuel with forty percent lower maintenance costs. All in all, the cash operation cost of the -300 is one-third less than that of the early-model 747s.

The -300 program launched in June 1995 and achieved firm configuration in October 1995. Boeing set an aggressive goal to enter the aircraft into service thirty-two months after firm configuration. The first scheduled delivery was to Cathay Pacific Airways of Hong Kong. "We chose the Boeing 777-300 because its capacity, operating economics, and range fill an important niche in our fleet requirements," said Peter Sutch, chairman of Cathay

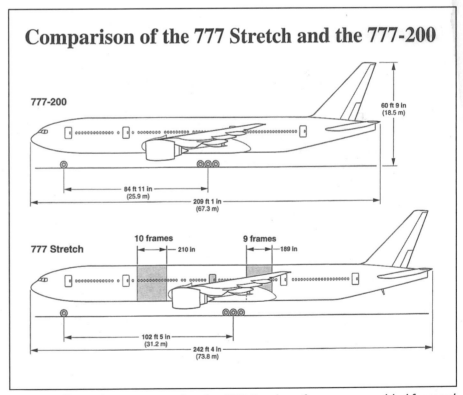

Comparison of the 777 Stretch and the 777-200

777-200

60 ft 9 in (18.5 m)

84 ft 11 in (25.9 m)

209 ft 1 in (67.3 m)

777 Stretch

10 frames — 210 in

9 frames — 189 in

102 ft 5 in (31.2 m)

242 ft 4 in (73.8 m)

777-300 dimensions compared to the -200. Fuselage frames were added forward and aft of the wing. (Boeing)

Costumed dancers lead the roll-out of the first 777-300 at the company's Everett, Washington factory. The dancers represented the various Asian cultures of the airline customers that have placed orders for the -300. (Boeing)

View of the -300 roll out ceremony emphasizing the 33-foot longer length of the latest version of the 777. The -300 has a twenty percent passenger increase over the -200. (Boeing)

Long length of the -300 is evident in this view. Flat shape of the tail cone, which houses the APU, is still a distinguishing feature for identifying a 777. The additional door over the wing is a method of identifying a -300. (Author)

The Boeing 777 aircraft family has captured more than sixty-seven percent of the market share for aircraft in its class since the program was launched in October 1990. As of August 15, 1997, Boeing had delivered eighty-five 777s to thirteen airlines. It has 323 announced orders for the aircraft from twenty-five airlines worldwide.

ADDITIONAL FEATURES OF THE 777-300

Length is the most obvious difference on the -300. In addition to increasing passenger load capability by 20 percent, length has driven several new features. It is the first production aircraft to use cameras as standard equipment. Because the -300 has the largest wheelbase in commercial flight, cameras are needed to show -300 pilots how close the wheels are to the edge of the taxiway or runway for better maneuvering.

The ground maneuver camera system provides vital views of the main and nose gear, providing situational

777-300 Flexible Seating

Economy class — 500 passengers

Dual class — 451 passengers
40 first class | 411 economy class

Tri-class — 368 passengers
30 first class | 84 business class | 254 economy class

Three examples of passenger seating arrangements for the -300. "Flex Zones" allow rearranging of the aircraft into many different seating combinations. (Boeing)

Ground maneuver camera on the bottom of the fuselage and aft of the nose gear. The line and cable are a reflection of items on the ground in the highly reflective aluminum. This is the first production aircraft use of a ground maneuver camera system. (Author)

awareness during taxi that is not available otherwise to the pilots. Three small cameras are mounted on the exterior of the aircraft. One is mounted on the bottom of the fuselage, housed in a compact aerodynamic housing that looks forward at the nose gear. Cameras in the left and right horizontal leading edges each look down and forward at the main landing gear. Compensation for the movement of the horizontal stabilizer is accomplished without moving parts. Electronic compensation saves weight and increases reliability.

The cameras are solid state electronic Charge-Coupled Devices (CCDs) produced by Ball Aerospace & Technologies Corporation. The video electronics unit gives the pilots a three-way split screen view of the gear. The image in the cockpit is on one of three multifunction displays, as selected by

Elements of the ground maneuver camera system, the nose camera, video interface unit, and the horizontal stabilizer camera. (Ball Aerospace & Technologies Corp)

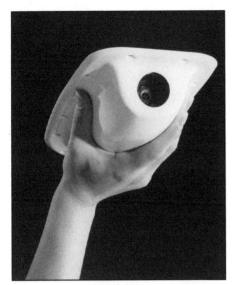

Compact nose-view camera of the ground maneuvering system. This CCD camera, in its aerodynamic enclosure, is one of three cameras used to provide a view of the landing gear to the pilot when taxiing on narrow taxiways. (Ball Aerospace & Technologies Corp)

The small circle in the leading edge of the horizontal stabilizer of the -300 is the ground maneuver video camera. Two horizontal stabilizer cameras in the left and right horizontal stabilizer look down and forward at the main landing gear. (Author)

the pilot. Camera light sensitivity covers the full range of operation, from night to bright sunlight.

This type of camera has potential for future use as part of the in-flight entertainment system. During flight, video from the cameras could be sent to the video interface unit and routed to the entertainment system. Passengers could access landscape views regardless of their seat location.

Because of the longer length of this aircraft, a production retractable tail skid has been added on the bottom of the fuselage. A replaceable shock absorbing crush cylinder is used in conjunction with the tail skid. For flight test, a hinged wand on the bottom of the fuselage sends a signal to the cockpit before tail contact occurs.

Two doors and evacuation slides, one on each side, have been added over the wing. Additional Flex Zones for the galley and lavatory were added. Structural changes for the -200 IGW are on the -300. Cargo capacity in the lower holds totals eight 96-inch-by-125-inch pallets, 20 LD-3 containers, and 600

Jeff Goedhard, right, test director on WB501 explains flight deck features of the -300 to the author. (Carol Upton)

cubic feet of bulk cargo, for a total available cargo volume of 7,080 cubic feet.

First flight of 777-300 WB501 occurred on October 16, 1997, taking off from Paine Field in Everett, Washington for a successful four-hour flight

ending at Boeing Field in Seattle. Frank Santoni, 777-300 chief pilot and John Cashman, chief pilot for Boeing Commercial Airplane Group, flew first flight. WB501 is powered by Rolls Royce Trent 892 engines, one of three

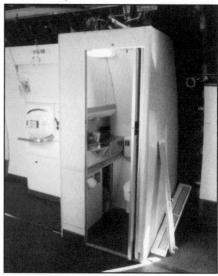

"Flex Zone" lavatory in the -300 is one of the items retained in the cabin during flight test. Structural and plumbing provisions for the "flex zones" allow moving galleys and lavatories to locations to accommodate seat rearrangements. (Author)

engines being tested on the -300. The other two engines are the Pratt & Whitney PW4090 and PW4098. A total of six aircraft will be used in the flight test program, which will encompass over 1400 hours of flight test and certification flying.

Three test aircraft are powered by Rolls Royce engines and three are powered by Pratt & Whitney engines. As of November 15, 1997 the first three -300's were flying out of the Boeing Field flight test center. Cliff Moore, Director of Flight Test Engineering for the Boeing Commercial Airplane Group said "Using multiple instrumented airplanes in the -300 Flight Test Program allows us to complete flight test in a shorter time span. The Rolls Royce Trent 892 powered -300 is scheduled for completion of testing and FAA certification in May 1998, with scheduled delivery to Cathay Pacific Airways later that same month."

The -300 will undergo the same flight tests run on the 777-200, as discussed in Chapter Three of this book. Pratt & Whitney powered -300 certification is expected in June, 1998 for the PW4090, and September 1998 for the PW4098.

A production retractable tail skid is one of the new items for the -300. The tail skid extends and retracts at the same time as the landing gear. (Author)

WB501 during preflight preparation for the October 16, 1997 first flight. This is the first of six aircraft that will be used in the flight test program for the -300. (Author)

Trailing static cone line coming from the tip of the vertical stabilizer is visible in this view. Notice the rudder tab. (Author)

Successful "Working Together" philosophy is carried on with the -300. (Author)

WB501, the first 777-300, is powered by Rolls-Royce Trent 892 engines. Two more flight test aircraft will be Rolls-Royce powered and another three will be Pratt & Whitney powered. (Author)

Aft fuselage view of WB501 during preflight preparation. Flap mechanism fairings can be seen at the top of the photo. (Author)

Early installation photo of the flight test water ballast system in the -300. Notice the overhead structure prior to installation of the cabin trim. (Boeing)

Forward water ballast and instrumentation racks in WB 501. Partial cabin trim and luggage compartments have been installed in the first flight test aircraft. (Author)

Flight test airborne data system in the -300. Consoles are used for in-flight monitoring and analysis of the flight test data. (Author)

777 Range Capability From Los Angeles

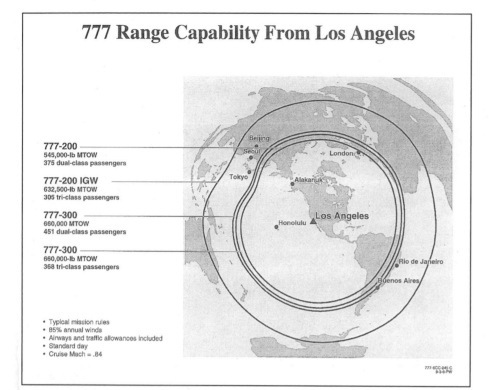

777-200
545,000-lb MTOW
375 dual-class passengers

777-200 IGW
632,500-lb MTOW
305 tri-class passengers

777-300
660,000 MTOW
451 dual-class passengers

777-300
660,000-lb MTOW
368 tri-class passengers

Beijing
Seoul
London
Tokyo
Alakanuk
Honolulu
Los Angeles
Rio de Janeiro
Buenos Aires

• Typical mission rules
• 85% annual winds
• Airways and traffic allowances included
• Standard day
• Cruise Mach = .84

777-6CC-245 C
9-3-6-PW

Aircraft range comparison of the 777 family. Ranges are shown from Los Angeles. (Boeing)

First flight take off of the 777-300 at Paine Field in Everett Washington on October 16, 1997. Flight was flown by 777-300 chief pilot Frank Santoni and chief pilot for Boeing Commercial Airplane Group John Cashman. (Boeing/Tom Hansor)

THE FUTURE

This book has discussed the Boeing 777 family as it currently exists: initial -200, longer-range -200 IGW (Increased Gross Weight), and stretched -300. At the aircraft's initial roll out on April, 9, 1994, Phil Condit, President of the Boeing Company, described the 777 as a thirty to fifty year venture.

Some future versions being studied:

777-100X

Shorter, truncated variations of the -300. One -100X study would have six fuselage frames removed. This aircraft would have about a 632,500-pound maximum takeoff weight and would require 90,000 pound thrust engines. Total fuselage length would be 44 feet shorter than the -300X and 10.5 feet shorter than

the -200X. The aircraft would carry 271 passengers in three classes for a total of 7,625 nautical miles.

In another -100X study, the -300 would have 12 frames removed, and the fuselage would be 54.3 feet shorter. With a projected 660,000-pound maximum take-off weight, this -100X could have a range up to 8,420 nautical miles carrying 250 passengers.

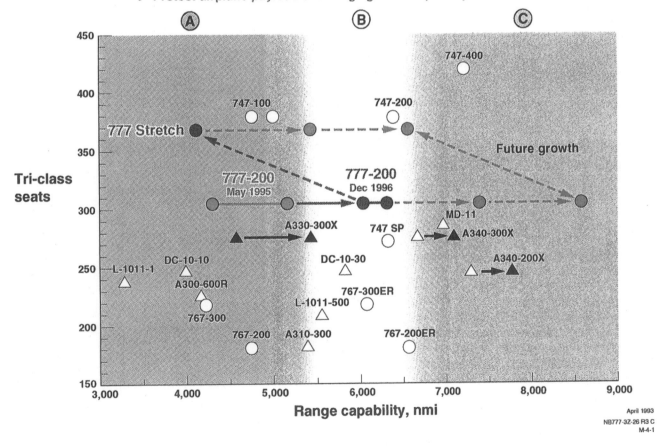

777 family objectives compared to other airliners. Objectives include increasing both range and seating capacity. (Boeing)

Emissions testing of a GE90-92B engine at the GE Aircraft Engines test complex near Peebles, Ohio is another example of the type of testing that is done long before a new engine makes its first flight. (GE Aircraft Engines)

Icing tests, in this spectacular night photo of a GE90 high bypass turbofan engine, are representative of the testing that is done prior to flight and for future development models of the GE90 engines. (GE Aircraft Engines)

777-200X

An ultra long range version. In studies, the -200X would use the wing, landing gear, and cockpit of the -300, as well as higher thrust engines. A 660,000-pound maximum takeoff weight would require engines with up to a 93,000 pound thrust rating. Other changes would include strengthened vertical fin and body sections. This -200X would have a range of up to 7,455 nautical miles carrying 298 passengers in three classes.

Another -200X study with a 690,000-pound maximum takeoff weight would use a strengthened landing gear, -300 wings, and be powered by engines with up to a 98,000-pound thrust rating. Extended wing tanks would add 1,460 gallons to the fuel totals. Structural strengthening and new rudder power control units would also be used. This -200X would have a range of up to 7,970 nautical miles carrying 298 passengers in three classes.

Malaysia Airlines signed a memorandum of understanding with Boeing on March 4, 1997. The company will be among the launch customers for an ultra long range 777-200X.

777-300X

Another study. The -300X has an increased gross weight to 690,000-pounds maximum takeoff weight (up from 660,000-pounds) with a range of 6700 nautical miles. 777 cargo versions are also being looked at in various studies.

FOLDING WING TIP

Folding wing tips are an interesting option that has not, to date, been selected by any of the airlines. Originally proposed by American Airlines, this concept could be a solution to tight gate space (the 777 has a 199 foot 11 inch wing span). The mechanism design was similar to that used by U.S. Navy carrier aircraft. Engineering design and prototype construction were completed, but not flight tested. The folding wing tips weighed about 3000 pounds.

LOWER DECK USES

Studies of other uses for the lower deck have included flight attendant rest modules with a main deck entrance that could accommodate up to ten peo-

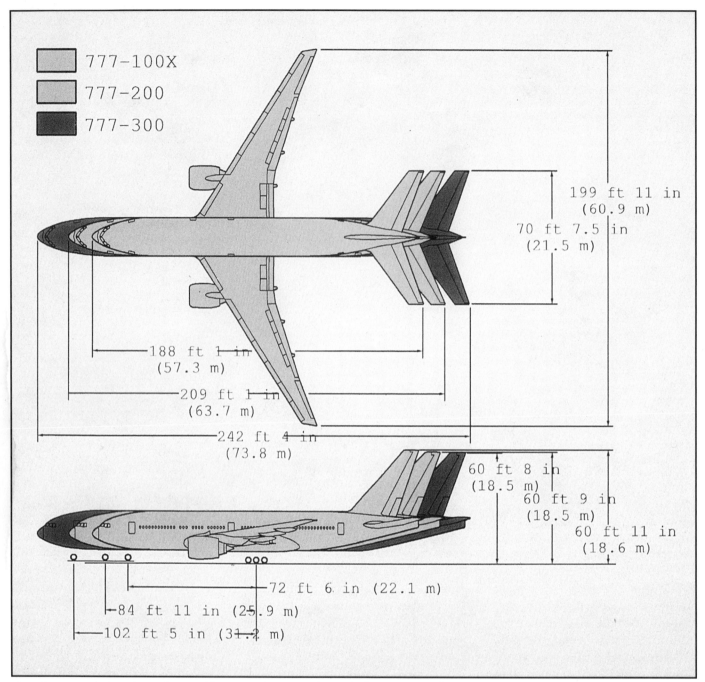

777-100X
777-200
777-300

199 ft 11 in
(60.9 m)

70 ft 7.5 in
(21.5 m)

188 ft 1 in
(57.3 m)

209 ft 1 in
(63.7 m)

242 ft 4 in
(73.8 m)

60 ft 8 in
(18.5 m)

60 ft 9 in
(18.5 m)

60 ft 11 in
(18.6 m)

72 ft 6 in (22.1 m)

84 ft 11 in (25.9 m)

102 ft 5 in (31.2 m)

Drawing comparing sizes of a -100X, -200 and -300 study. With the -300 now flying, a shorter version of the 777 seems likely as the next step. (Boeing)

ple. A modular lower-lobe passenger sleeping compartment would have eighty-two and eighty-six inch long berths with an aisle height of about sixty-three inches. With a lowered floor variant, it could accommodate a person 76 inches tall. Up to forty beds and a lavatory could be installed in the forward hold.

FUTURE ENGINES

As the aircraft changes, propulsion requirements usually follow. The three engine manufacturers designed growth provisions into their respective engines. Boeing engine requirements for the 777X versions ranged from 90,000-pound thrust versions of the Pratt & Whitney 4090, General Electric GE-90-90B and Rolls Royce Trent 890 for the 777-300 through possible 93,000-pound and 98,000-pound derivatives.

All three manufacturers have higher thrust rated engines in development or the process of certification. Pratt & Whitneyís PW4098, with a takeoff thrust of 98,000 pounds, is under development. It is planned for certification in January 1998. General

Engine flight testing of a GE90-92B, mounted on the inboard location on the left wing of the GE 747 flying testbed. This is a 92,0000 lb thrust version of the GE90 engine. (GE Aircraft Engines)

Electric has a 102,000 pound thrust version of the GE90 engine. As of June 1997, General Electric Aircraft Engines (GEAE) was delaying certification of this engine until a suitable market develops. They are continuing to validate technology for an engine with more than 100,000 pounds thrust while they further refine the engine requirements, and gauge market interest. GEAE will be ready to proceed when an acceptable market emerges for this engine. The Rolls Royce Trent 8102 is designed as a 102,000 pound thrust growth version of the Trent 892 engine. The 892 is rated at 92,000 pounds thrust and has been run at thrusts exceeding 114,500 pounds during development testing.

With many potential new versions being studied, the Boeing 777 is sure to be around in the future. Market driven, this aircraft is built to respond to the customer's needs.

APPENDICES

BOEING 777 ANNOUNCED ORDERS

AIRLINE	-200	-300	ENGINES
Air China	5		Pratt & Whitney
AIR FRANCE	10		General Electric
All Nippon Airways	16	12	Pratt & Whitney
American Airlines	7		Not yet determined
Asiana	7	8	Pratt & Whitney
British Airways	23		General Electric
Cathay Pacific	4	7	Rolls-Royce
China Southern	6		General Electric
Continental	5		General Electric
Egyptair	3		Pratt & Whitney
Emirates	9		Rolls-Royce
Garuda Indonesia	6		Not yet determined
GE Capital Aviation Services	5		General Electric
ILFC	34		General Electric
Japan Air System	7		Pratt & Whitney
Japan Airlines	10	5	Pratt & Whitney
Korean Air Lines	4	8	Pratt & Whitney
Kuwait Airways	2		General Electric
Lauda Air	4		General Electric
Malaysia Airlines	11	4	Rolls-Royce
Saudia	23		General Electric
Singapore Airlines	34	2	Rolls-Royce
South African Airways	4		Not yet determined
Thai Airways	8	6	Rolls-Royce
United Airlines	36		Pratt & Whitney

TOTAL 777-200's ORDERED - 283
TOTAL 777-300's ORDERED - 52
TOTAL announced orders - 325

TOTAL CUSTOMERS - 25

BOEING 777 PRODUCTION LIST

Line	MSN	Model	Reg.	Airline	1st Flight	Delivery	Engine	Notes
1	27116	-200	N7771	-----	06/12/94	-----	PW	Owned by Boeing
2	26936	-222	N774UA	UAL	08/03/94	03/29/96	PW	*Customer Greg Milano*, ex-N7772
3	26932	-222	N771UA	UAL	08/02/94	11/27/95	PW	*Frank Griffith Customer*, ex-N7773
4	26929	-222	N773UA	UAL	10/28/94	01/31/96	PW	*Richard H. Loung Customer*, ex-N7774
5	26930	-222	N772UA	UAL	11/19/94	09/29/95	PW	*Mary Beth Loesch Customer*
6	27105	-236	G-AAAA	BA	02/02/95	05/20/96	GE	*Sir Frank Whittle*, ex-N77779
7	26916	-222	N777UA	UAL	04/25/95	05/15/95	PW	*Working Together*
8	26917	-222	N766UA	UAL	05/04/95	05/24/95	PW	*Nancy J. Meyer Customer*, ex-N77776
9	26918	-222	N767UA	UAL	05/17/95	05/31/95	PW	*Sam Sotoodeh Customer*
10	27106	-236	G-ZZZB	BA	04/11/95	03/28/97	GE	*Sir William Sefton Brancker*, ex-N77771
11	26919	-222	N768UA	UAL	05/31/95	06/26/95	PW	*Marcelo Amodeo Customer*, ex-N77775
12	26921	-222	N769UA	UAL	06/13/95	06/28/95	PW	*D. Timothy Tammany Customer*, ex-N77773
13	26925	-222	N770UA	UAL	06/26/95	07/13/95	PW	*Thomas R. Stuker Customer*, ex-N7772
14	27265	-267	B-HNA	CPA	05/26/95	08/23/96	RR	ex-N77772, ex-VR-HNA
15	27107	-236	G-ZZZC	BA	09/01/95	11/11/95	GE	*Sir Charles Edward Kingsford-Smith*, ex-N5014K
16	27027	-281	JA8197	JAL	08/31/95	10/04/95	PW	lsf Sumishin Leasing, ex-N5016R
17	27108	-236	G-ZZZD	BA	11/19/95	12/28/95	GE	*Orville Wright/Wilbur Wright*
18	27266	-267	B-HNB	CPA	11/09/95	10/25/96	RR	ex-N77773, ex-VR-HNB
19	27109	-236	G-ZZZE	BA	12/03/95	01/12/96	GE	*Sir John Alcok/Air Arthur Whitten-Brown*
20	27257	-21B	B-2051	CZ	11/30/95	12/28/95	GE	
21	27028	-281	JA8198	ANA	12/09/95	12/21/95	PW	lsf Sumishin Leasing
22	26947	-222	N775UA	UAL	01/07/96	01/22/96	PW	*Scott A. Neumeyer Customer*
23	27364	-246	JA8981	JAL	01/26/96	02/15/96	PW	*Sirius*
24	27358	-21B	B-2052	CZ	02/09/96	02/28/96	GE	ex-N5107V
25	27726	-2D7	HS-TJA	THA	03/01/96	03/31/96	RR	*Lamphun*
26	27365	-246	JA8982	JAL	03/08/96	03/28/96	PW	*Vega*
27	26937	-222	N776UA	UAL	03/22/96	04/11/96	PW	
28	27263	-267	B-HNC	CPA	04/04/96	05/09/96	RR	ex-VR-HNC
29	27029	-281	JA8199	ANA	05/02/96	05/23/96	PW	lsf Sumishin Leasing
30	27247	-21H	A6-EMD	EK	05/02/96	06/04/96	RR	

Line	MSN	Model	Reg.	Airline	1st Flight	Delivery	Engine	Notes
31	27264	-267	B-HND	CPA	05/22/96	06/13/96	RR	ex-VR-HND
32	27727	-2D7	HS-TJB	THA	05/30/96	06/13/96	RR	*Uthai Thani*
33	27248	-21H	A6-EME	EK	06/14/96	07/03/96	RR	
34	26940	-222	N778US	UAL	06/27/96	07/18/96	PW	
35	26941	-222	N779UA	UAL	07/10/96	07/26/96	PW	
36	26944	-222	N780UA	UAL	07/17/96	08/06/96	PW	*Spirit of Adalyn*
37	27030	-281	JA8967	ANA	07/26/96	08/12/96	PW	
38	27031	-281	JA8968	ANA	08/02/96	08/14/96	PW	lsf Diamond Lease
39	27366	-246	JA8983	JAL	08/15/96	09/12/96	PW	Altair
40	26945	-222	N781UA	UAL	08/23/96	09/12/96	PW	
41	27483	-236B	G-VIIA	BA	10/04/96	07/03/97	GE	ex-N5022E, "Waves of the City" color scheme
42	27249	-21H	A6-EMF	EK	09/25/96	10/16/96	RR	
43	26939	-222B	N787UA	UAL	10/29/96	06/05/97	PW	
44	27728	-2D7	HS-TJC	THA	10/07/96	10/25/96	RR	*Nakhon Nayok*
45	27636	-289	JA8977	JAS	10/23/96	12/03/96	GE	
46	27359	-21B	B-2053	CZ	10/29/96	11/15/96	GE	
47	27250	-21HB	A6-EMG	EK	11/21/96	07/25/97	RR	ex-N5028Y
48	27360	-21B	B-2054	CZ	11/15/96	12/05/96	GE	
49	27484	-236B	G-VIIB	BA	12/06/96	05/23/97	GE	ex-N5023Q
50	27032	-281	JA8969	ANA	11/27/96	12/16/96	PW	
51	27729	-2D7	HSTJD	THA	12/10/96	12/19/96	RR	*Mukdahan*
52	26938	-222B	N786UA	UAL	03/23/97	04/04/97	PW	
53	27485	-236B	G-VIIC	BA	01/08/97	02/06/97	GE	ex-N5016R
54	27251	-21H	A6-EMH	EK	04/22/97	05/15/97	RR	
55	27524	-21B	B-2055	CZ	01/29/97	02/28/97	GE	
56	27486	-236	G-VIID	BA	02/03/97	02/18/97	GE	
57	26948	-222B	N782UA	UAL	02/14/97	03/07/97	PW	
58	27487	-236	G-VIIE	BA	02/14/97	02/27/97	GE	
59	27945	-2B5B	HL7530	KAL	03/04/97	03/21/97	PW	
60	26950	-222B	N783UA	UAL	02/24/97	03/11/97	PW	
61	27488	-236B	G-VIIF	BA	03/03/97	03/18/97	GE	
62	27946	-2B5B	HL7531	KAL	03/14/97	03/28/97	PW	
63	27252	-21H	A6-EMI	EK	03/14/97	04/11/97	RR	ex-N5020K
64	28408	-2H6	9M-MRA	MH	03/26/97	04/23/97	RR	ex-N5017V, round-the-world record – 03/31-04/02/97
65	27489	-236B	G-VIIG	BA	03/31/97	04/09/97	GE	
66	27525	-21B	B-2056	CZ	03/31/97	04/18/97	GE	
67	28507	-212B	9V-SQA	SQ	04/11/97	05/05/97	RR	
68	27651	-246	JA8984	JAL	04/11/97	04/21/97	PW	Betelguese
69	26951	-222	N784UA	UAL	04/16/97	04/29/97	PW	
70	27490	-236B	G-VIIH	BA	04/23/97	05/07/97	GE	
71	28423	-266B	SU-GBP	MS	05/05/97	05/23/97	PW	*Nefertiti*
72	27652	-246	JA8985	JAL	05/02/97	05/14/97	PW	Procyon
73	26954	-222B	N785UA	UAL	05/07/97	05/21/97	PW	
74	28409	-2H6	9M-MRB	MH	05/16/97	05/30/97	RR	ex-N50217
75	27033	-281	JA702A	ANA	06/10/97	06/30/97	PW	
76	27491	-236	G-RAES	BA	05/30/97	06/10/97	PW	"Delftblue Daybreak" color scheme
77	27938	-281	JA701A	ANA	06/09/97	06/23/97	PW	
78	28410	-2H6B	9M-MRC	MH	06/09/97	06/24/97	RR	
79	27637	-289	JA8978	ANA	06/18/97	06/26/97	PW	
80	28424	-266B	SU-GBR	MS	06/24/97	07/02/97	PW	*Nefertari*
81	27034	-281	JA703A	ANA	07/09/97	08/21/97	PW	ex-N50217
82	26942	-222B	N788UA	UAL	07/08/97	07/15/97	PW	
83	28508	-212B	9V-SQB	SQ	07/07/97	07/18/97	RR	*Jubilee*
84	28411	-2H6B	9M-MRD	MH	07/17/97	07/30/97	RR	
85	28425	-266B	SU-GBS	MS	07/18/97	08/07/97	PW	*Queen Tiye*
86	28509	-212B	9V-SQC	SQ	07/30/97	08/06/97	RR	
87	28698	-2Z9	OE-LPA	NG	07/23/97	09/24/97	GE	ex-N5022E
88	26935	-222	N789UA	UAL	07/31/97	08/11/97	PW	
89	27730	-2D7	HS-TJE	THA	08/04/97	08/15/97	RR	*Chaiyaphum*
90	28510	-212	9V-SQD	SQ	08/25/97	09/11/97	RR	
91	27253	-21HB	A6-EMJ	EK	08/25/97	09/30/97	RR	
92	26943	-222	N790UA	UAL	08/15/97	08/28/97	PW	
93	26933	-222	N791UA	UAL	08/21/97	08/28/97	PW	
94	27507	-367	B-HNE	CPA	10/16/97	-----	RR	First 777-300 (expected delivery May 1998) Test reg. N5018K
95	27731	-2D7	HS-TJF	THA	09/18/97	09/29/97	RR	*Pahnom Sarakham*
96	26934	-222	N792UA	UAL	09/14/97	09/25/97	PW	
97	26946	-222B	N793UA	UAL	09/22/97	10/07/97	PW	
98	28344	-268B	HZ-AKA	SVA	10/28/97	12/29/97	GE	
99	28345	-268B	HZ-AKB	SVA	10/21/97	12/27/97	GE	ex-N5023Q
100	27732	-2D7	HS-TJG	THA	10/22/97	10/11/97	RR	*Pattani*

Notes: "B" = Increased Gross Weight (IGW). Engines: GE – General Electric GE90-92B; PW – Pratt & Whitney PW 4084; RR – Rolls Royce Trent 871. Airlines: ANA – All Nippon Airways; BA – British Airways; CPA – Cathay Pacific; CZ – China Southern Airlines; EK – Emirates; JAL – Japan Airlines; KAL – Korean Air; MH – Malaysia Airlines; MS – Egypt Air; NG – Lauda Air; SQ – Singapore Airlines; SVA – Saudi Arabian Airlines; THA – Thai Airways International; UAL – United Airlines. Lsf: leased from.

Table courtesy Airliners Magazine, P.O. Box 521238, Miami, FL 33152-1238

SIGNIFICANT DATES

OCTOBER 1990
United Airlines announces the largest wide-bodied aircraft order in aviation history and becomes the launch customer for the Boeing 777 at the same time. The agreement includes orders for 34 777's and 34 options. On October 29, Boeing's board of directors makes the launch official.

November 1990
The New Airplane Division officially becomes the 777 Division.

December 1990
All Nippon Airways becomes the -777's second customer for 15 777s and options on an additional 10.

February 1991
Full scale 777 interior-cabin sales mock-up is unveiled at the Boeing plant in Renton, Washington.

March 1991
Completion of the aircraft's first-phase configuration definition. The eighth IBM mainframe computer to support 777 CATIA users is installed. The eight connected mainframe computers represent the largest mainframe cluster in the world.

May 1991
Construction begins on the 518,000 square foot Integrated Aircraft Systems Laboratory in Seattle. The -777 will be the first to use the new lab. Boeing signs a final agreement with Japanese airframe manufacturers to build approximately 20 percent of the 777 airframe structure.

August 1991
British Airways, another of the airlines instrumental in configuring the 777, places firm orders for 15 777's with options for 15 more. The airline selects GE90 engines for its 777's.

October 1991
All Nippon Airways selects Pratt & Whitney's engines to power its 777's, while Thai Airways International selects the Rolls Royce Trent 800 engine.

Japan Airlines announces its decision to order 20 777's including firm orders and options.

December 1991
Lauda Air orders four-longer range 777's for delivery in fall 1997.

21 January 1993
Major assembly of the 777 starts.

9 April 1994
Ceremonial roll out of the 777.

12 June 1994
First flight of the 777 at Paine Field in Everett, Washington.

19 April 1995
FAA/JAA type design and FAA production certification for the 777.

15 May 1995
First delivery of the 777.

30 May 1995
FAA ETOPS approval for the 777.

7 June 1995
First revenue service flight.

14 June 1995
Boeing's 777 digital design process earns the 1995 Computerworld Smithsonian Award for top spot in the Manufacturing category.

15 February 1996
The Boeing 777 twinjet named the winner of National Aeronautic Association's 1995 Collier Trophy for "designing, manufacturing, and placing into service the world's most technologically advanced airline transport".

15 November 1996
The 777 development team receives the National Air & Space Museum Smithsonian Institution Achievement Award for "reshaping the way the industry builds airplanes by developing 'working together' relationships with the airlines, partners, suppliers, and all who designed and built the 777 to create the most advanced and service-ready twinjet in commercial aviation history.

April 1997
The 777-200 IGW breaks FAI world speed and distance records for flying the fastest and farthest of its size and class on a flight from Seattle to Kuala Lumpur, Malaysia.

8 September 1997
Roll out of the -300 stretched version of the 777 at Everett, Washington.

16 October 1997
First flight of the 777-300 at Paine Field Everett, Washington.